THE EFFECTIVE STUDENT

The Effective Student

A CONSTRUCTIVE METHOD OF STUDY

H. Chandler Elliott, M.A., Ph.D.

PROFESSOR OF ANATOMY, NEUROLOGY, AND PSYCHOLOGY
UNIVERSITY OF NEBRASKA COLLEGE OF MEDICINE

HARPER & ROW, PUBLISHERS
NEW YORK, EVANSTON, AND LONDON

This book is gratefully dedicated
to my teachers, colleagues, and
students, all of whom have contributed.

FIRST EDITION

LIBRARY OF CONGRESS CATALOG CARD NUMBER: 66–20762

H-Q

Contents

Introduction

A friend of mine once told how he paid for a set of lessons to improve his bridge game. During the first lesson, he realized, with a shock, that he was stalling like a bored school boy: "Uh-huh, uh-huh. Yes, I see," with his mind out the window. Of course, he pulled himself up short with: "You poor chump, this is *your* baby," and buckled down.

I will assume that study is your baby for whatever reason—ambition, interest, or just necessity. My object is not to arouse your efforts but to organize, economize, and direct them—even to moderate them where they are excessive; I only tell you how to carry the baby.

I. Who

The book is addressed to students who want to be effective, not to instructors or parents. Obviously, it will reach mainly those who are interested enough in their work to take thought about how to do it. Of these, it addresses four groups:

The failing and marginal student: Seventy-five per cent of scholastic failure is due simply to poor study and examination techniques. Indolence, distracting personal problems, uncongenial subjects, or (rarely) inability, take their toll. But most failures work hard, suffer only normal distractions, could appreciate their subjects, and are potentially competent. Only, their efforts are misdirected.

The passing but inadequate student: This largest group fails to realize its full potential even with hard work. Most such people take for granted that you drudge ahead and get by. Yet almost all of them could raise their standing considerably with far less backbreaking toil and far more satisfaction.

The good but not-good-enough student: Even more tragic is the wastage of human potential in such cases, because they are capable of so much. Yet they are the hardest to reach: After all, one can hardly improve on an A standing, can one? True. But is the standing still below potential, rated by low standards, and achieved at the cost of overdriven drudgery? To aid one of these people is a high privilege.

Students in practical life: People after graduation are less likely to realize the need for effective study than are school and college students. But often they need it even more: Their time is more limited and irregular; their competition is more intense; and their facilities and aids are less adequate. Yet few people above the level of laborer or minor employee (and many below it if they are ambitious) can escape study in the modern world. Even if they do not take night-school or extension classes, they must follow trade and professional journals, learn new methods and data, and refresh old ones; and the better they do this, the better for them. In the modern world, every intelligent person must be a student throughout life. So, I would hope, this book may find its way to people in many walks of life outside the classroom. Its emphasis on self-reliance should be of particular value to such readers. And perhaps it will be introduced to others, by those who keep it at hand as a trusty friend rather than banish it to the attic after graduation. It might even make its greatest contribution in the wider world.*

* A recent study of adult education has come to hand as this book was being prepared for the printer. The following comments from it are of interest here: Experts estimate that a person in any sort of skilled profession or trade will require a retraining period every five or six years, about seven times in a forty-year career. Others require more education to qualify for better jobs. Many wish simply to put to better use the leisure that is now becoming so widespread as to be almost a problem. Altogether, in the United States almost 30 million adults, about a quarter of the adult population, are currently enrolled in some form of regular study. This amount of "post-school" education is greater than I myself had realized. And the need for effective study techniques is correspondingly broadened.

For guides to sources of adult education, see Chapter 1, footnote p. 12.

II. How

Until recently, most people took study methods for granted and left them to instinct. Realization that studying *how* to study should come before everything else is spreading in the world of education. Skill in this subject can multiply efficiency in all others.

This book presents a system for studying and for applying what has been learned, in examinations—and beyond. It has been written in the light of many sources, academic and practical, but will present only the conclusions and advice distilled from these. It is a working manual for students, not a discussion for theorists.

In such a manual, only the most basic problems and techniques can be covered. Every student has particular problems, and endless methods and variants of study are of value to different individuals. To collect and classify all these would only confuse everybody. The methods presented here, however, are basic. They have worked for 90 per cent of those who have used them, and they can be adapted by *anyone* with the initiative to seek out and apply them. Special techniques for varied types of subject will be given throughout the book; but even these are "special generalities."

In short, my aim is to leave the reader with a clear, simple plan of action, not an exhaustive and bewildering catalog of possibilities.

I have based this plan on my own student experience, which was disciplined by some outstanding instructors. I have tested and refined it in the course of extensive and varied studies since then. I have myself observed and analyzed the methods of thousands of students. And I have subjected the manuscript to the candid comments of many students, excellent or in difficulty. For a practical text, only practical qualifications are valid.

III. A Fatal Flaw

The method, however, has no built-in spell that compels you to carry it out. You may be convinced of its merits, even enthusiastic, and full of noble intentions to apply it—by and by, after you have finished your usual orgy of cramming for the next test or the like. In that case, believe it or not, the method will not work.

A discouraging example of this sad fact recently confronted me: A student came to me in grave concern about his standing, which certainly bordered on failure. I loaned him a copy of the manuscript for this book and waited with interest to see if his grades improved. But in fact, to my consternation, the grades fell farther, in spite of his earnest approval of the method. Apparently the method just did not work for him.

Then the puzzle was solved. At a further conference he naïvely confided to me his latest technique of "study"—naïvely, because he had evidently quite overlooked my disparagement of this technique (page 47). With all the solemnity of a child who had found a four-leaf clover, he told how he had acquired a *special pencil* for underlining (or coloring over) passages that struck him as important; then, he said, he went over these passages again and always got them better on the second reading. No doubt two readings helped him more than one, but obviously (to anyone but himself) not enough to save him on examinations. Since he had already received more than his fair share of the attention I had to give to problem students, he was left to his folly with a reproof and a sigh. And he continued on his collision course.

I cannot stand over you even to that degree but can only thus admonish you. After the first appeal that led to your buying the book, you are on your own, unless you have the great asset of some other person to needle you. Indeed, an excellent insurance for getting results, here or anywhere, is to put yourself on record with someone whom you respect, who understands what you are doing, and who will have enough interest to check up on you. In this way, you can reinforce your own determination to really apply the method.

First, however, make up your mind that this method is no magic formula for "success without sweat." In fact, it will demand that you work as perhaps you have never worked before. True, it should cut down the actual hours of drudgery and boredom; but it will pack the fewer hours with concentrated, organized effort that you may find rather exacting at first. If you are willing to hold on and give the method a fair trial, experience has shown that you will soon begin to enjoy the satisfaction of success as you may not have thought possible. If you are not resolved on such a trial, we had better part company here.

The book is in three sections. The first covers preliminaries and accessories to study; it clears away the brushwood that is so often a major obstacle to effective work. The second gives a program for actual work, organized both broadly and in detail; this is, of course, the heart of the book and will command your most careful and frequent attention. The third part discusses the techniques of applying your knowledge effectively in examinations. To save time and effort, the book should be read first from start to finish; that is how it is planned. Only after that should you pick out special parts for your special needs.

PART I

Study Aids and Accessories

Raw Material Is Important:
Books, People, and Schools

Much difficulty in study is due to unsuitable study sources. The study material provided by authority is usually taken for granted by the student. But a critical evaluation of this material may pay rich dividends. This is, of course, more often true at higher education levels. But even an enterprising high-school student can often profit greatly from the following advice.

Efficiency of learning depends on clarity of the material to be learned—that is, clarity to *you*. You cannot, indeed, expect any textbook or instructor to be 100 per cent clear: If the subject could be reduced to ABC, it would not need a school or college course to cover it. So, if your sources of material are reasonably clear to you, you may not need to seek farther for something impossibly simple. But if your sources really baffle you, a few hours' search for better ones can save you many days of fruitless toil. And even a good textbook can usually be supplemented to your great advantage.

Books and Other Publications

Of all study resources, these are the most easily changed and supplemented.

You may object to this. A text, you say, has been prescribed and will be used as the basis for examinations; and surely one book is as much as you can cope with.

As for examinations: In most subjects, all authoritative texts cover much the same ground, the chief difference being in style of presentation. In state- or nationwide examinations for professional standing, candidates from many schools, usually taught from a variety of texts, answer the same questions with about the same percentage of success. A text must simply be adequate.

As for "extra" books: If the "one" book is obviously giving you serious trouble, you are wasting time, effort, and appreciation of the subject. Another book may save you much of the wasted time, only a fraction of which need be paid back in checking for differences from the prescribed text—a procedure that is often profitable in itself. And a change of textbook may make the work far more pleasurable and your grasp of the subject more vigorous.

Even if the prescribed text is not too bad, another book may be valuable. It can give you fresh points of view, challenge your critical sense by comparison, and relieve the boredom of going over and over the same old script when reviewing. Two eyes can judge better than one.

In any case, decide carefully what you need. Do not just go looking around vaguely for "something better than this piece of junk."

The trouble may be in the book, or it may be in you. Perhaps both book and you are good enough but ill matched. Think: Which is the real situation in your case?

The commonest *fault with textbooks,* especially advanced, is ponderousness. In many subjects where information could formerly be covered by a small book, a massive tome is now needed. Instructors frequently prescribe such a tome so that their students will have a source of future reference; and they intend to bring out the essentials, the bones of the subject, in lecture. Unfortunately, even with good lecture courses, the textbook must be called on frequently, and the massive tome is clumsy and discouraging. In that case, one needs either a more concise book or one in which major themes are clearly distinguished.

The commonest *fault of students* when they find a book burdensome is inadequate background. This will be dealt with later (page (68) but the right book, to compensate for the lack, is our interest here. Of course, if one simply has not mastered preliminary subjects, a quick refresher review may be the only solution. More often, the information is in the student's mind, but its use, in the bewildering new field, is obscure and confused. Here again, a simple introductory book, or one sympathetically written, may be priceless.

For example, I recently had to acquire some knowledge of modern biochemistry and found it a mass of baffling detail. But a pair of "popular" books by a well-known authority gave me a foundation that surprised my biochemical colleagues. From this beginning, I was able to proceed to what I wanted in more technical books, efficiently and with appreciation. I even enjoyed those two little books, though I am supposed to be an advanced scientist. So you need not be ashamed to follow suit.

To find books and other material, major and supplementary, you have a variety of sources that may surprise you.

1. *Libraries* are too seldom used, and are even more seldom used effectively. Even a high-school library, and much more a college or university library, should contain a wealth of alternative texts and of enlightening, stimulating background material. Nor should the public library be disdained, especially if you want sources to liven up a subject. Librarians, too, are often neglected by bashful, hasty, or simply uninformed seekers; yet these librarians have entered their profession out of interest in books and in helping people to find the right ones. So, a library can be used best under professional guidance.

You should, however, do some original hunting, since only you know exactly what you want. An excellent *Guide to the Use of Books and Libraries* can be consulted in many libraries by anyone who expects to be doing more than a little book-hunting. A visit to the stacks in person, where you can sample books freely and quickly, is a revealing experience if permitted. And you should make a practice of surveying topics in the card index, with an eye to picking out plums. A little experience will make you a good judge of what is worth examining further. And scanning stacks and index is a habit that can serve you well throughout life.

2. *Interlibrary loans* are a means of getting books you very much want. A college or university library can get you such books, not on their shelves, from larger or more specialized libraries. (It cannot, however, borrow a book that is still in print—i.e., that it could buy for itself.) This service usually costs only postage, which is not much for books, and is less trouble than you might think. But of course, it cannot be overworked for trifles.

3. *Other people* besides librarians can very often guide you to good books: a sympathetic instructor, professional friends and acquaintances (see People, below), knowledgeable classmates or upperclassmen, or indeed, almost any informed person. As with librarians, just don't be bashful.

4. *Bookstores* are a resource not often thought of. Though he may not stock the special books you need, the bookseller is usually a person of broad information and has access to more reference sources and book lists than even the libraries. On a recent project, I requested my bookstore to provide me with lists of nonfiction paperbacks. They responded with a package of folders that took me an afternoon to scan, and yielded a score of valuable titles at minimum cost. These, of course, I could keep and annotate as I could not do with library books.

5. Files of *semipopular magazines* may present lucid, stimulating articles. One such article may open out a whole subject to you and turn drudgery into fascinated insight. In my own field, *Scientific American* and *American Scientist* publish always readable, yet authoritative, articles not only on the physical and biological sciences, but on sociology, psychology, history, etc. Newspapers are notoriously unreliable for serious information, but some, such as the *Christian Science Monitor,* the *Wall Street Journal,* or the *National Observer* often publish reports that are models of clarity and accuracy. *Reader's Digest* provides endless, compact source material. Even technical journals often contain well-written, revealing, inspiring articles.

But how do you find the right articles in the jungle of material? *The Reader's Guide to Periodical Literature,* available in most large, general libraries, indexes the more popular sources. *The International Index to Periodicals* covers more scholarly sources. And special fields, such as medicine, engineering, and law, have their guides to really technical material. Ask your librarian about these, and don't hesitate to enlist her aid in using them.

One caution is appropriate here: You will find that the semipopular journals are full of alluring articles on curious topics. When you are looking for specific material, do not let these distract you; don't leaf and browse, but consult tables of contents and indexes, look up only articles that seem relevant to your interest and promptly discard any, even of these, that prove unsatisfactory. Your time is too limited for side issues; if you spot something that really intrigues you, take it along for leisure reading. But don't mix business with amusement.

6. *Encyclopedias* often give a valuable bird's-eye view of a topic. True, many encyclopedia articles are dry and condensed, "dehydrated," and for reference, not for reading. But often they give you the framework, the "pattern" to be discussed later. Anyhow, if you have such a source handy, a few minutes should suffice to show if it has anything to offer you. And do not be satisfied with one; try all that are available: *Britannica, Americana,* and *Everyman's* are among the most notable; *Colliers* is more popular in presentation, but excellent. Encyclopedias of biography, sciences, and so on are also available.

7. If your project is long-term, you can get on the *mailing lists.* Write to publishers who specialize in your field—you can learn of these by simply looking at available books. A postcard requesting recent publications in "American history," "geology," or whatnot will be answered by a catalog and by further announcements— perhaps for years. Not only that, but other publishers may have access to a mailing list and will also send you catalogs and announcements. These may guide you to discoveries in the library; you may even persuade your library to acquire a book and so repay the publisher; or you may occasionally decide to get a book for yourself. In the latter case, however, try to look at a copy and make sure it fulfills your expectations before you order; books that sound exciting in a prospectus, or a dust-jacket blurb, may be in fact worthless to you. This general procedure is followed by many worldly-wise scholars.

8. The *Government Printing Office,* Division of Public Documents, Washington, D.C., 20402, will furnish fortnightly lists of new publications on endless topics, and lists of publications on special topics on request. Publications range from pamphlets to large books. The service is free, and the material is sold at cost.

All this is not to say that you should spend too much time looking for short cuts, "soft snaps," and the like. For real results, you must work on something solid. But a great majority of students are lamentably unenterprising and neglect the boundless opportunities to find both more nourishing "solids" and more appetizing "spices." Such students become hacks, not leaders.

What you need may be difficult to find. But bear in mind an old gypsy proverb: "The dog that trots around *finds* a bone." So if your studies are going badly, do not sit and grind yourself down on an unsatisfactory text. *Trot* around. Even if this takes hours away from grinding, you may save many, many times more. You may even transform grinding into sculpturing.

Judging Material for Yourself

Your finds from the foregoing sources may be an embarrassment of riches or a lone gold-piece. In any case, how do you judge whether a book is what you need without spending a lot of time? No one answer is sufficient.

1. First, of course, is *your own reaction:* Consult the book for topics that have given you trouble and see whether they are clearer to you. Try other, unfamiliar topics (familiar ones may seem easy because you have already broken the ground). Study a few illustrations, if there are any, and see whether they enlighten you. If all seems well, so far so good; but be more critical. Even a simple, introductory book should not be fiberless pap. It should challenge you.

2. Critically scan *practical features* of the book. (a) Does the *table of contents* show that the book covers the subject adequately? The table should preferably be not just a list of chapters but include subheadings, though this is not essential, especially in a small book. Anyway, is everything listed that you need? And is the table itself stimulating? If so, that is a good indication of a well-written book. (b) How about the *index?* In most subjects, any book intended for study should be thoroughly indexed. The quality of this feature is often a measure of the author's care and reliability. Does it seem adequately long and well arranged? Think of some reasonable but not too obvious terms and see if they are included. (c) How about *subheadings?* Are they well marked and sufficiently numerous? This feature may be of great help to you in study, as will be seen. It also indicates how thoughtfully the author has prepared his material for students. If you find an otherwise excellent book without subheadings, you can often gain much profit from supplying your own (Chapter 5). But lack of them is usually a warning signal. (d) Minor features are sometimes worth noticing. *Summaries* at the beginnings or ends of chapters can be very

helpful. *Questionnaires* at chapter ends are valuable, if they are good ones. Clear, full *legends for illustrations* save much work and are priceless for review. These and other things are not only good in themselves but an indication of good authorship in a textbook.

3. How about the *author?* If you are engaged in serious work, you want somebody of authority to guide you. The fly-leaf should give you not only an author's name but his titles, degrees, and, often, other publications. Good books are sometimes written by unknowns, especially introductory and popular-interest books: but a serious text should have solid authority. On the other hand, authoritative books are often, though not always, ponderous and heavily written. Try to find an authority who can also write well.

Make sure the author is not a crank or plugging some special point of view. You can usually spot this sort of thing early in a book. And although "cranks" sometimes turn out to be true prophets, and fresh points of view can be interesting, just now you are getting educated, not evangelized. Discard him.

4. Check the *date* of publication, usually noted somewhere on the title, copyright, or other such, page. Date matters less for a book on literature, history, and the like. It usually matters more in books on science, sociology, and the like. In some subjects, a book over ten years old is significantly out of date.*

No book is going to score 100 per cent on these counts. But you should look for the best before you invest money (and later, time) in a book.

People

People are a remarkably neglected source of aid. They can help you in a wide variety of ways.

---

* One notable exception to "outdated" books sometimes occurs. Real classics in a field, the original Great Books of a topic, can be amazingly lucid and vital: Works such as Parkman's books on American history, Gibbon's and Mommsen's on Roman. Hakluyt's on Elizabethan voyages; Isaac Newton's, Heaviside's, and Faraday's in physics; Osler's, Lister's, and a host of other original workers in medicine; and so on in practically every subject. Of course, new work has always been done since these giants wrote; but it has built on, not replaced, them. To read such works is often not only a practical aid but an inspiration, such as is mentioned in Chapter 6. They are, compared to later paraphrases, like paintings to black-and-white photographs.

1. *Teachers outside of class:* These, of course, vary greatly in their attitudes, but most are willing to help a serious questioner. Routine teaching, especially after years of repetition, tends to become monotonous, and a student with a special problem may even be welcomed as a change. But go with a definite question, not with a general complaint that you do not understand the subject; someone who is willing to help with a knotty problem may not be ready to give you a complete private review course unless he is very generous. And do not go with a question on some point so obscure that it looks as if you were trying to "stump teacher"; this is a good way to make yourself unpopular. Don't be bashful, but do be tactful, and put yourself in the teacher's place.

2. *Experts, professional, and other:* Most people with special knowledge are flattered by appeals for information and can sometimes make things clearer than any book or academic instructor. A professional electrician once cleared up in five minutes, with a pencil sketch and a plain explanation, a point in electronics that had been bothering and delaying me for a month. You may not always find the expert you want; but if you take an interest in people around you, you will find a surprising wealth of information freely at your disposal. A habit of consulting experts is one thing that helps to make leaders. But, again, apply the recommendations given above for teachers, and especially use tact.

3. *Classmates:* Two heads are usually better than one, and several are sure to be better still—if congenial. Informal chats at lunch or evening bull sessions certainly should often serve as pure relaxation and escape from "shop"—of which relaxation I am a strong advocate. But impromptu discussion of some study subject, at such times, may show it to be unexpectedly amusing, reveal fresh viewpoints, stimulate thought by disagreement and argument, or (at the very least) let you see that you are not alone in your difficulties. The lone wolf loses these sources of knowledge and stimulation. If you pick up good points in this way, make a habit of jotting them down as soon as you can do so inconspicuously— you do not want to look like a square or a brain-picker. Otherwise such gems often elude you later: "What was that neat point John made?"

4. *Study groups:* In contrast to casual discussion, these are deliberately organized with the serious intention of doing effective

work during legitimate work-time. Such groups can be a very powerful help to their members: A working trio of myself and two friends was the most valuable influence on my college career. The recommendations for study sessions given in Chapter 13 are easier to apply in a group, which enforces a desirable but not galling discipline. Especially when preparing for modern "objective" examinations, group work is almost indispensable, as will be described (Chapter 16).

But before getting into such a group, make sure that it *will* be congenial and serious in its aims. If at least one member is a little (but not too much) better than you, you are likely to profit; on the other hand, explaining things to a weaker student may clarify and fix them in your mind as nothing else can do. Of course, group work should not exclude private study or even, in most cases, outweigh it.

5. *Tutoring:* This is a heroic measure only occasionally useful; but sometimes it can save an otherwise lost cause. It is bound to be expensive if the tutor is any good; and even an expensive tutor can be unsatisfactory. The best way of finding someone worthwhile is to inquire of qualified people: your teachers, your principal, your acquaintances in school and out. Do not advertise or answer ads; you will be working blind and can be badly victimized. You should always try to find some former pupil of the tutor and get his opinion on the quality of the help given.

Even with the best recommendations, avoid engaging the tutor for a long contract. Start with a fair trial run, so that you can see whether he will be worth his cost. If he is not, have some diplomatic excuse ready for not continuing with him. In high school, because of health problems, I had three different tutors. Two of these not only advanced me in particular subjects but introduced me to methods and attitudes that have been of great profit to me ever since (page 81); one was completely worthless and was dropped in short order. Here, as elsewhere, you must learn to judge and act in your own interests.

6. *Tutorial schools:* Of these, often called "cram schools," I cannot speak from experience. They seem to do a good job, since they remain in business; and they may be less expensive than a private tutor, though you are usually required to subscribe for a whole course. Again you should, if possible, get the opinions of qualified people and former students. Such schools can be corre-

spondence or "live," the former requiring more self-discipline and resolution. Again, use your judgment.

Schools and Other Institutions

In the matter of regular schools, one has less freedom of choice. Nevertheless, one is seldom absolutely tied to a bad situation.

Poor teachers occur in every school. They may completely spoil a subject for you, if you let them; but you need not. In senior high school I had one teacher whose failing was his concentration on a few star pupils to the neglect of the rest of us. Thus thrown on my own resources, I used some of the devices given here and below, and discovered the satisfaction of self-reliance. Before the college entrance examinations, this man patronizingly told me, "Just keep your head, Elliott, and you should get through." I *did* get through —and took a scholarship, including one in his subject, over the heads of some of his pets. The same can apply to incompetent, confusing, and other types of poor teachers.

Really *poor schools* are fortunately rare. But when they do occur the problem may be serious. Below college level one is more or less obliged to attend his district school; but not absolutely. In extreme cases, something can usually be done if your family co-operates. You can generally make do with a poor school, as with a poor teacher, by organized private enterprise. If you can afford it, a private school may be the answer; only, be sure the school is worth the expense and change of curriculum. Make the same inquiries as you would about a tutor or cram school, only even more thoroughly. If you cannot manage such a school, a determined campaign by your family may get you transferred to some other reasonably near regular school on some pretext or other; I have seen it done in three cases. Let me warn that one of these cases entailed a certain amount of unpleasantness for the student when word got around that he was transferring, though the other two were simply taken for granted. But pleasant or not, you do not want to cripple your scholastic and future career by putting up with uncongenial, unprofitable, or substandard school facilities. Make up your mind (and your family's), set your course, and stick to it.

With *colleges* and other *institutions of higher learning,* an ounce of prevention is worth a pound of cure. You almost always have a choice. Unfortunately, few people realize just how wide a choice they do have, but take a line of least resistance. Choice of a college is a big subject, far beyond the scope of this book. But many sources of information and guidance are available:

1. *Lovejoy's College Guide,* sold in bookstores, gives concise, vital information on just about every such institution of any standing in the United States and dependencies, as well as much general advice; *Comparative Guide to American Colleges, For Students, Parents, and Counselors,* by James Cass and Max Birnbaum, is also of great value.

2. *American Universities and Colleges,* published by the American Council on Education, Washington, D.C., 20436, is encyclopedic, and might best be consulted at a library.

3. The Government Printing Office (see page 6) will send you a list of its publications in the field, which can be had very cheaply.

4. *Changing Times* (Editors Park, Maryland, 20782), a magazine of useful and reliable information on practical topics, runs a monthly feature on schools and colleges, as well as occasional articles; and it will supply reprints of some earlier articles for a small charge.

5. Or you may look up articles on the subject in the *Reader's Guide to Periodical Literature.*

6. In special fields, the AAMC (American Association of Medical Colleges, 2530 Ridge Avenue, Evanston, Illinois), for example, publishes an annual review of member colleges with more detailed information than is given in *Lovejoy.* And other professions have similar sources of information.*

---

* As noted in the Introduction, adult education is now a major and rapidly growing activity. How can you find the facilities for it (aside from full-time enrollment)?

1. Your *local schools* usually have adult programs for academic credit, job training, or recreation. A simple phone call to school principal, guidance counselor, or board of education should inform you on possibilities.

2. Most *colleges and universities* have evening, week-end, and other adult courses leading to degrees and diplomas, or simply for cultural purposes. The college registrar's office should be contacted for information.

3. If the foregoing facilities are inaccessible or are inadequate for your needs, *correspondence courses* are available in great variety. (a) The *commercial* type, mentioned above, tends to be more practical and technical, though not exclusively. Such schools are listed in the *Directory of Accredited Home Study Schools,* available free from the National Home Study Council, 1601 Eighteenth Street, NW, Washington, D.C., 20009; (b) The *college extension* type covers just about every subject imaginable. To find where you can get what you want, consult *A Guide to Correspondence Study in Colleges and Universities,* available for 50 cents from the National University

With all available data in your hands, you may discover possibilities you had never dreamed of. You may then be able to make a wise choice on the bases of personal preferences, reputation of faculty members, opinions of attending students, finance, and so on. A really thorough research may take quite a bit of time and energy. But this is well worth while if it results in four or more years of maximum accomplishment rather than of dissatisfaction.

In Sum

You are not bound down to any unsatisfactory source of education. You live in a world of wide variety and should learn to take full advantage of it. By this means alone, you can hardly fail to improve your performance, sometimes very greatly.

You have boundless sources of written material: alternate texts, libraries of many sorts, bookstores, magazines for every taste and guides to them, encyclopedias, publishers, and the government printing office.

You can learn to judge this material by critical examination of its substance and accessory features.

You can draw on a possibly unexpected variety of personal help.

You can cope with poor teachers and even poor schools. And you have a wealth of guides to the wide choices of higher education.

Extension Association, 122 Social Science Building, University of Minnesota, Minneapolis, 55455.

Workshop and Tools:
Study Place and Study Aids

This chapter is included on student advice. Its subject seemed to me so obvious that I decided to omit it, but was emphatically dissuaded by those reading the rough draft. So here it is: a discussion of study place and equipment.

I will later advise you to use odd times and opportunities for study, wherever you are. But that is advanced technique, which can be made effective only after establishing the basic study habits to be described. To establish those habits, the best of conditions are called for. And a familiar, well-equipped place of work is needed for most study.

Student circumstances differ for almost every individual. Almost anyone, however, can fulfill minimum requirements with a little determination; the remaining few unfortunates should at least try to meet as many of those requirements as possible. Here, obviously, we can discuss only general types of situation.

Place of Work

Freedom from distractions is the first requirement of study quarters.

1. *Distractions from without* naturally spring to mind first: loitering associates, telephone calls, family members with their own problems or recreations, and so on. These can be dealt with

best not by saying "Get thee behind me, Satan" monotonously, but by keeping out of Satan's way. If you are in the library or some similar inaccessible place, or simply insist you are not available for bull sessions or telephone calls between certain hours, you can make it stick; and you are far less likely to be considered a prig, and more likely to be respected, than if you have to keep repeating, "No." Build a fortress, real or virtual.

Such a fortress can range from a room of one's own with a latchable door, through the college library with its enforced quiet and atmosphere of study, a fraternity or residence study room, a room with an ambitious or at least co-operative companion, to a corner of the basement or attic suitably equipped. If you are studying intensively, the elegance or bleakness of your surroundings won't matter.

2. But *self-made distractions* must also be dealt with. A fortress is of small use if you smuggle little, personal devils into it yourself. The newspaper, the daydream-inducing souvenir or photo, the entertaining books, the hobby material, and such, have their place. That place is not your work-bench.

The most universal of self-made distractions is the radio. Indeed, it is claimed by some students as a necessary accompaniment to study—"I can concentrate better *with* it," said smugly. This is akin to the assertion: "I drive *more* carefully after a drink." In part it may be a juvenile pose; and in part, it may have become a need very like that of the drug addict who feels lost without his continuous stimulant, which is similarly injurious to real self-command. So far as I know, no serious research has been made on the effect of radio on study achievement; but careful research *has* been done on the similar situation of people who sleep in noisy surroundings. They did sleep *seemingly* well but, by scientific test, not well at all. And (I will lay very long odds), the same is probably true of the cherished habit of studying to a distracting background of radio noise. Such a petty, self-handicapping indulgence or pose is not worthy of anyone with mature motives.

3. *Breaks* in an intensive study session are a good thing. Your fortress should not become a dungeon. I strongly advocate the cup of coffee, the phone call, the brief visit, and so on, to refresh your energies (Chapter 4). But they should be out of sight and mind during study, and enjoyed *away* from your work-room, where they will have the added advantage of making you get up and stir your

circulation when you are ready for them. Let them be *breaks,* not ever-present distractions.

Working Conditions

Having selected your fortress, you furnish it. Of course if you work at the library, or such, many things are arranged for you, well or badly; but you can still do a good deal by picking a quiet corner with good light and so on. If you work on your own, your freedom and responsibilities are wider.

In this connection, I recall a cartoon I saw many years ago: A hobo was sitting in the blazing sun, obviously very uncomfortable, with sweat streaming down his face. He was eyeing a tree some ten yards away and lamenting, "Boy oh boy, I'd give *any*thing to be sitting in the shade of that tree." This struck me as so funny, and has remained in my mind so long, because it illustrates a universal human weakness—tolerance of discomfort from sheer inertia. How often do you penalize your efficiency in similar, if less obvious, ways?

1. *Lighting* is taken for granted by many people. They either tamely accept what they find or follow some conventional plan. Ten minutes' experimenting in this matter may greatly improve your working comfort and, so, your efficiency. Authorities constantly recommend sufficiently bright light; but this may be misapplied or overdone. For example, students often complain that many textbooks have glossy paper which reflects light and causes eyestrain headache, cutting down performance. Yet this can always be eliminated by placing the light sensibly. ("Boy oh boy, I'd give *any*thing . . .")

Therefore, pay attention to (a) proper strength of illumination—that is, the strength *you* find comfortable; (b) position of light—it should illuminate but not reflect, and should light the desk but not shine in your face (frosted bulbs are always better for study); (c) a light that you can readily adjust for different purposes; and (d) an arrangement that does not get in your way and can be removed entirely when you want space. If your lamp cannot be made to do these things, use initiative and get one that can. Obvious solution, yet often disregarded.

2. *Seating* is equally important, and equally often neglected.

The test here is simple: When you turn your attention to it, does your chair make you in the least uncomfortable? The same chair will not suit the tall and the short, the plump and the lean; it may fit one person satisfactorily but afflict another with a continuous mild discomfort that slyly bleeds his energies. In my department, our teaching laboratory provides simple uniform stools which must be tolerated by students during classes; but when students study there at night, I have seen them fidgeting, hunched up, perched on the edge of the stool, tilted over the desk, and so forth, though a roomful of comparatively comfortable chairs is available next door—and is used by the wiser ones. ("Boy oh boy, I'd give *any*thing . . .")

If your chair does not permit an unstrained posture, and another is not available, a few minutes will suffice you to saw half an inch off the legs or to add it by means of spiked-on feet; a couple of dollars will provide a foam-rubber pad; inconvenient arms can be removed. An easy-chair or bed is pleasant for casual reading, but only an upright chair permits active work. You will have to spend many hours with it; so, see that it is an asset, not a liability.

3. *Desk* is usually another taken-for-granted item—a desk is a desk is a desk, and you use what you have. For many years, I typed at home on a small desk-table; but one day I realized tardily that after a couple of hours of such typing, I had a stiffness and fatigue of shoulders and neck the next day. A quick check showed that the table was nearly two inches higher than my typing table at college. When I sawed over two inches off the legs, I found work far less tiring and, in fact, lost a subconscious tendency to shirk or cut short work at that desk. Really, it was now better, because half an inch lower, than my college typing table. The latter could not be lowered, having metal legs and wheels, but a thicker chair pad improved matters there too. So, for years, "Boy oh boy, I'd have given *any*thing . . ."

Organization

1. A *disorganized desk* is like a muddy path clogging progress. Consider the following horrible example catalogued from real-life observation: a table strewn with heaps of notes, reference books buried in the underbrush, pencils, scratch paper, textbooks, cata-

logs, an unhandy table-lamp, a clumsy pen-stand, ashtrays, an empty coffee cup, a half-empty cigarette box, the beginnings of a term paper in a folder, a portable typewriter, a useless blotting pad, a half-spilled box of paper clips, more notes, scattered rubber bands, colored ballpoints, a photo in a frame, a couple of weight-less paperweights, a desk calendar with an unused memo pad, a petrified rubber, some odd letters "to be answered when he got around to it," some hobby magazines to browse in when his mind wandered, and an address book. This was hardly a good place for work.

For one thing, it ensured that he continually wasted time hunting for things that should have been promptly to hand when he wanted them. For another, it was a mine of distractions. For a third, it discouraged him from making useful references and notes because the materials were a nuisance to find. But even worse was the effect on his morale; the shambles confronted him with proof that he was an incompetent goof and encouraged him to behave as such. He admitted all this and agreed that he needed to prove otherwise. (I do not know if he did.)

2. *The ideal layout* is the most austere possible. In a commer-cial establishment, the small fry (who are going to remain small fry) follow the cluttered-desk plan as far as regulations permit; the minor executives have in-out baskets and less rubbish; the big boss probably has a large, shiny* desk top with a phone and sophisticated lamp, across which he can impress visitors and on which he lays out the work of the moment—with a battery of organized drawers in easy reach. Maybe you cannot go that far, but you might keep the picture in mind: the less on the desk, the better.

Organize. Banish everything, no matter how cherished, that does not relate directly to the work in hand. If you have drawers, ruthlessly clean out all the rubbish that has collected in them and set aside useful articles for processing. Then put your secretarial accessories—pencils, clips, rubber, etc.—in a shallow drawer, preferably in small topless boxes that will keep them roughly sorted.

Papers should be in file folders. Ordinary cardboard folders are

* A shiny top, however, is better for impressing visitors than for study. It glares and adds to eyestrain.

cheap and should be stocked in quantity so that you need not waste time making fresh purchases. Used and battered folders should be thrown away—re-use is false economy. Folders should be labeled on the tabs, on the front, and, at least by a word, on the back. If you have not a drawer that holds your folders conveniently, why not a cardboard carton of convenient size to be kept handy yet out of the way? Make it a strict rule to put every folder back *in place* when you have finished with it. The saving in time can be material.

These are merely illustrative suggestions. You will probably have other ideas that work for you. But however you do it, make a business of organizing your place of work. The feeling of release, and the real increase in efficiency, will delight you.

Accessories

These will naturally vary with individual needs: an engineering, a high-school, and a medical student will need quite different accessories. But some pointers do apply to most people.

First, *keep it simple*. If you need two colored ballpoints for annotating (page 48), don't get half a dozen. If you need crayons, don't luxuriate in an artist's set of twenty-four colors—of which you will wear three or four down to stubs without ever resharpening the others. An old friend once ruefully showed me a slide rule he had acquired in college, a magnificent thing with a dozen scales and an accompanying manual; he had used the simpler scales briefly in a few courses and, since graduation, had taken square and cube roots a few times; he could have done as well with a simple pocket instrument such as the rest of us bought. Human nature is often tempted by glitter. Resist, less for economy than for efficiency.

1. A *typewriter* is a common study accessory even for high-school students. Used typewriters can often be had very cheaply. A ramshackle machine, however, is not a bargain at any price; it will wear you out with exasperation and delays for repairs, and produce inferior typescript that can seriously downgrade the impression your work makes. Good reconditioned typewriters are sold by most typewriter and office-supply companies with even a guarantee. (The longer the guarantee, the less likelihood of trouble—the

sellers are sure it *won't* come back for repair.) Portables are cheaper and are convenient for many student purposes beyond routine.

Unless in constant use, the machine should be out of the way. In its case, under the desk, it will not hamper you and will collect no dust. If on the desk, it can sit back under the overdesk shelf, which should be designed accordingly.

2. *Typewriter accessories* can double or halve the value of your machine.

Typing paper is of many qualities. If you want to economize, by all means use cheap grades or even scrap for rough work. But do not economize falsely on final drafts. A paper called corrasable bond allows you to erase errors without a trace left; this may cost you as much extra, on a fifty-page theme, as a package of cigarettes; and it will shape up into a smart, impressive manuscript. Other methods of correction are far inferior.

An *eraser* that erases cleanly is needed even for corrasable bond.

Carbon paper and *copy paper* (or just a pad of scrap) are musts. *Never* type anything of importance, even in rough draft, without making a carbon copy. One lost or destroyed manuscript without a surviving copy can cause you more trouble than ten years of making copies. Besides, if you want to refer to some manuscript that is in someone else's hands, there is your copy.

Typewriter ribbons should never be worked to exhaustion. A faint, gray typescript is infuriating to a reader. To avoid the temptation of running a ribbon too long, always have a spare handy.

3. A *reading-stand* can be a big help to anyone. It is not only useful for reading: It keeps a book out of the way, yet clearly visible, while you consult it as you write, or keeps a frequently used reference book handy while you read another book. It can solve the glossy-paper problem by putting the book at an angle where it does not reflect—especially if the lamp is placed *behind* it and bent to shine down on the book but not into your eyes. It can hold manuscript conveniently, at an easy angle for reading, when you are retyping.

The stand should not be cumbersome but should be sturdy enough to hold your biggest books; and it should have a projecting support at the bottom, adequate not only to support the book but to hold open stiff new books and tightly bound journals and yet not hamper page-turning—a simple, broad, uptilted ledge is as good as anything. Lightweight, adjustable, collapsible reading-stands are too prone to collapse and will not hold books open. Heavy wire, or plain, homemade wooden articles are probably best.*

4. A *stapler* may or may not be rated among the excess baggage deplored above. If you are handling quantities of papers in small lots too numerous to rate separate file folders, the stapler may prevent disastrous confusion. In such cases, paper clips tend to come off or to interlock with other sheaves of paper, and a staple is more permanent. On the other hand, you should never use staples on manuscript intended for survey by others. You should see for yourself what a nuisance this can be; indeed, some editors refuse to consider stapled manuscripts, and many teachers would like to do the same—hence staples do not improve your standing with authority. If you do need a stapler for your own use, this is one item where oversimplicity may be false economy: Cheap, light staplers won't handle more than a few pages, and quickly go out of order. If you feel the stapler is worth getting at all, get a sturdy but not fancy model.

5. A *shelf* over the desk can keep books handy yet out of the way. Two or three bricks at each end and a plank with strong end-pieces (so the books will not be continually flopping in inconvenient piles) can suffice. Now you can make quick references by a reach of the hand without the mental shirking of the effort involved in rummaging. A small, sturdy, upright box on the shelf can hold small paperback reference books and pamphlets.

6. The *books* should include those, and *only* those, that you use in active work: texts, dictionaries, special reference books, and such. Any book used only occasionally should be in a convenient bookcase.

Keep spares of items that need renewing: pencil leads, ink, paper, carbon paper, staples, ballpoint fillers, and such. This habit may save an evening's work now and then. When a spare is used,

* A workable makeshift is one of those gritty, adhesive strips used in bathtubs to prevent slipping. Stuck to a desk top, with typewriter or other solid object for a back rest, such a strip will prevent even a heavy book from sliding down, and will permit easy page-turning. It cannot, of course, be adjusted freely and does not permit easy back-lighting. But it would be ideal for a limited space where a solid rest might be unhandy, or for a temporary work-place.

make a note of it, and replace *it* at the first opportunity. The satisfaction of slipping, say, a new cartridge into your ballpoint without a hitch, reflects good technique.

This list merely gives illustrative examples from personal experience and observation. It should be adapted to individual needs and might be extended indefinitely; but it would extend into more and more specialized items—medical, engineering, etc. Much of what is said above sets the tone for your decision as to whether or not you need other items and, if you do, what sort you should get. But in any case, isn't such a careful selection more effective than the dingy confusion described on page 17?

In Sum

Think and take pride in the organization of your study-place and equipment. It pays off in quicker, easier work, in less wasted time, in freer use of resources, and in self-confidence.

Your study-place should be planned for minimum distraction.

It should be furnished for efficiency—comfortable in all possible ways but not lazy.

It should, especially its desk, be cleared for action.

Its accessories should be adequate but streamlined, and good but not superfluous.

Human Aids:

Instructors, Lectures, and Notes

The custom of lecturing, when you come to think of it, is an odd one. Why, with a wealth of printed material available, and when most people learn better by eye than by ear, is so much time consumed giving and taking lectures? At the great English universities of Oxford and Cambridge, students do most of their own studying guided only by periodic interviews with a "tutor." Lectures are special, occasional events, usually by outstanding authorities. Judging by cultured Englishmen, the system works admirably. However, readers of this book live in a world of increasing mass education and are sure to be subjected to a great deal of lecturing. How, then, can the situation be turned to best advantage?

The following advice applies chiefly to higher levels of education and to certain groups of subjects—notably those called the humanities, medical and biological work, and other descriptive science, less so for mathematics and related fields, languages, and applied sciences. However, it is valid for much high-school work and for almost any subject, with simple, suitable, and sensible adjustments. Since readers of this book are presumed to be enterprising, details of such adjustments are left to them.

How Not to Do It

Bad technique in taking lectures (aside from inattention, fatigue, inadequate preparation, and other ways of merely *exposing* oneself to the sound of words) can be summed up in one word: *scribblemania*.

This is a currently fashionable, almost universal practice. It consists of sitting through a lecture with no apparent object in mind but to write down as much as possible of what the lecturer says. The brain acts merely as a computer converting audible symbols into written symbols; or perhaps it is haunted by dim recollections, questions, or ideas, but has no leisure to formulate these. Any thought, much less learning, must wait till the daily recording session is over—at which time most of the questions and ideas are gone forever in the avalanche of busy-work. But a procedure such as this is not justified simply because it is universal, even if a fair proportion of its devotees seem to do well enough in spite of it. In fact, scribblemania is a deplorable perversion of study, a major source of ineffective education and lowered standards. If you do not believe me, here are some reasons for my statement.

1. Scribblemania is an appalling *waster of time*. Lectures often occupy up to an average of 20 hours a week, 800 in a forty-week academic year, 100 eight-hour days! Most of this great output is utterly wasted by the student as inefficient stenographer, working furiously but learning almost nothing—merely preparing to learn something later. (Stenographers notoriously fail to register mentally what they transcribe.) An hour after lecture, most students would be hard-put to recall 10 per cent, much less 25 per cent, of the essentials in the lecture. Material presented in lectures immediately preceding an examination is, if given on the examination, miserably handled on the average, in spite of its supposed freshness; it has not been "really studied" by most of the class.

2. Scribblemania produces *paltry results*. "Good notes" are widely regarded with almost superstitious reverence as a magic talisman of success. Why? They are usually no more than a sort of accessory textbook—amateur, incomplete, and often incoherent. An overly conscientious student may waste further hundreds of hours "transcribing" the notes into a neat but still inadequate form; by which he learns very little and puts off actual learning for yet another stage. What a meager return for a major expenditure of time!

3. Scribblemania is indulged in for *ignominious reasons*. One of these is sheeplike compulsion—a feeilng that if you drudge hard

enough, like everyone else, you must be right, however profitless the work. Once, in the hope of encouraging and enabling my class to listen and learn during lectures, I mimeographed and distributed an outline of headings and subheadings, with space to jot down (literally) noteworthy points; but I saw the same rows of heads bent hypnotically over notebooks, the same feverish twiddle of pens. Later inspection revealed that the notebooks contained the same headings as did the disdained mimeographs, though not as complete or well arranged. No matter: Those students had fulfilled the ritual, sacrificed to the gods, and were ready to meet the normal, rather dull, standard. A small minority did use the outlines as intended, interlining special comments, queries, and such, in the space provided. To do this, they had to attend and think, recording on brain rather than on paper. All the really good students whose notes I peeked at were in this minority.

Another poor reason for scribblemania is insecurity, lack of self-confidence. If you get it *all* down, you have Good Notes and are Safe—more or less. Probably this insecurity is justified, and will continue to justify itself in a vicious circle. But real security comes from justifiable self-confidence, not from wasteful toil. You need to cut free from the deadening formula.

4. Scribblemania does not even *achieve its purpose.* Tradition goes: "You gotta give the guy [lecturer] back what he says." True, in many cases. But you are not going to do this by slavish stenography. Copying down routine material lends it no magic virtue; you can find it just as well, or better, in your textbook. You are merely burying "the guy's" real points.

How to Gain Maximum Profit from Lecture Time

Instead of this senseless procedure, determine to profit from your lecturer to the full *then* and *there.* Concentrate, and acquire the real meat of the lecture, recording only essentials and opening your mind to meaning. Just what should you hope to gain from a good lecture?

1. *Headings,* yes. You need these to indicate where points fall in the pattern of the lecture and course. You can readily detect major headings and subheadings in any competent lecture (if the lecturer is incompetent, masses of notes won't help anyway). Beyond this, do not bother: excessive sub- and sub-subheading is

usually not a guide but a burden. Anyway, your own organization (page 76) will be more useful to you.

2. Under the headings, what? (a) Any *points* that strike you as *new, original,* or of *special significance* according to the lecturer, including original numbered lists of points, tables, and special diagrams; (b) any *illustrative cases* not in your textbook, though not mere anecdotes; (c) memos of any *questions that remain unanswered,* or unclearly answered, of *ideas* to check, of *hopeful leads;* (d) any *comments* that seem to point towards *possible examination questions:* "You should be thoroughly familiar with . . . ," "The topic can be summed up for future reference in . . . ," and similar hints. You should learn to make adequate memos of such points without overwriting, or losing the thread of discourse.

But remember: If it is in the book, why labor to write it down?

3. But how do you recognize the "new and original" points, the unanswered questions, or simply just what is "in the book" or not? By the highly effective technique of *pre-reading.* You are going to read your text several times anyway; and you will gain powerful advantage if you make your first reading one jump ahead of, not one or several jumps behind, the lecturer: First, your reading will be more alert and focused as you anticipate matching it with the lecture. And second, having read the book, you will be alert and focused on the lecture itself, looking for the special points you want to glean. Prereading is the heart of effective lecture attendance and note-taking. Prereading for a lecture should be carried out as a "unit" (Chapter 10).

4. Every note-taker adopts certain *short cuts.* These usually accumulate more or less unsystematically as time goes on. An odd half-hour or two spent on organizing and expanding them, and then revising them in the light of experience, can be not only valuable but rather amusing. Ingenuity is always fun.

Note however, that these techniques should help you to write *less,* not more—the same condensed material in less space. If your object were to write more, some form of real shorthand, or a tape recorder, would be the solution. But this never works: Aside from transcription problems, it merely adds to the mass of superfluous material to be sifted and organized, and confuses the vital pattern. I know this from personal experience; and I do not know of anyone who has profited from stenographic lecture notes. No: The value of short cuts is to minimize distraction from the thread of the lecture. (See also discussion of handwriting on page 148).

5. Now, having reduced your note-taking to essentials, what do you do with the lecture time? You *challenge* the lecture. That is, you actively respond to the lecturer, continually demanding in your mind: "What does he *mean* by that? . . . Where does *that* fit in? . . . Is it essential or a digression? . . . He said 'four points' and he's only made three, or was such-and-such intended for the fourth? . . . That's not what the book said, or am I wrong? . . . Isn't he going to discuss . . . ?" And so on.

6. During parts of the lecture that are dull because you already know them, practice flash-back. Review mentally the outline of what has been said and what is likely to follow. Place yourself in the pattern.

7. At the other extreme, to sit idly through the lecture, as if hoping to record by sheer force of will, is folly. A few very gifted or highly trained people can do this: I remember one old lady who could repeat long and (to me) tedious sermons in great detail without notes. But most of us need to record at least highlights, so as to keep our minds from wandering, guide memory later, and provide a frame of reference for more special points. The entirely noteless student usually wastes lecture time as badly as the scribble-maniac. Judicious compromise is as important here as everywhere.

To switch from the habitual fifty-minute scribble may not be easy. Besides conventional habit and insecurity, compulsive note-taking is encouraged by what is really laziness in spite of the busy-work involved. Active attention to the lecture, an attempt to grasp essentials *then* and *there,* is tiring to unpracticed minds. It does not come all at once.

Yet the effort is very well worth making. Think of those hundreds of hours a year salvaged from mechanical toil and applied to real learning. Not that you will often carry away a perfect formal abstract of any lecture. But you should, because you are focusing, get a strong, vital impression. You will catch the spark, the inspiration from a good lecturer, find yourself ahead of a poor one, and get the real meat in any case. You will have your memos on special points, and your outline. And the knack improves enormously with average determination.

The contrast between drudge and thinker is universal: A famous painting by Rembrandt shows an anatomy class, a group of bearded, lace-ruffed, Renaissance Dutchmen following a demonstration by a dignified professor. Most of the class seems complacent, but in the forefront are two outstanding figures: One is leaning forwards, beard stuck out, gaze glued to the dissection as if trying to photograph every detail, significant or not, on his mind—note-taking was evidently not yet in vogue; the other has raised his eyes and, with almost visibly moving lips, is obviously asking himself, "Now why . . . ? And if so, what does that *mean* and how do I *apply* it?" Rembrandt, an artist, has characterized the first man with an earnest, honest, but rather stupid face, the second with a refined, almost spiritual one. In real life, you cannot always pick the types like that; but the types persist, and their achievements differ in class and even more in the outer world.

Rounding Out Your Notes

Even selective notes often fall short of satisfaction. The lecturer leaves questions unanswered, even omits what you feel to be vital or at least interesting points, or is unusually obscure. What should you do?

1. *Questions during lecture* are very problematic. If the lecturer is amiable, the class small enough so that questions from a fair percentage would not become burdensome, and your neighbors too seem baffled by an important discussion, you may elect to "bell the cat." If so, strive to be courteous and diplomatic:

> It is the duty of the student
> Without exception to be prudent.
> If wiser than his teacher, tact
> Impels him to conceal the fact.

Time your question so as not to interrupt a train of thought and yet not be far out of context. A raised hand allows the lecturer to choose his time. Always imply that the need for the question is due to your own shortcomings, not those of the lecturer: "I'm afraid I missed your point on such-and-such, sir. Would you mind repeating that?" Even so, reserve mid-lecture questions for rare and serious occasions. You have other resources.

2. *After-lecture questions* are a very different matter. You have a perfect right, even a duty, to ask them; and the instructor should be glad to receive proof of interest in his subject. (Personally, I find that students ask far too few, rather than too many questions,

though their examination performances show that this is not due to sublime mastery of the subject.) Many students seem to feel that exposing their ignorance will weigh against them, and sit mum in their corners with their problems and desperation. Yet the business of a teacher is to teach, and any that I know would rather be putting someone on the right track than carrying on dead routines. The only thing that does count against you is bad performance on examinations. So, *ask*.

The best *time* to ask questions, of course, is right after lecture while the topic is warm and the context clear. But use horse sense: If your man is obviously tired or hurried, you are not likely to receive the best response to your curiosity. In that case, say, "Dr. So-and-so, I'd like to ask you about a point when you have the time. When would it be convenient for you?" Remember, even though you are only asking him to carry out the more challenging part of his job, courtesy is always appreciated.

3. But never pester a busy man with *trivia* or things you could easily look up for yourself. At college, I had a professor nicknamed Luke; a Scot with a broad accent, he would often reply to questions with: "Did ye luke in the buke?" If you had "luked" and in vain, he was generous with his counsel; but usually he knew that the answer was available "in the buke" to anyone worth his salt, and felt that spoon-feeding was an imposition on him. All lecturers would approve of his attitude even if they do not share his bluntness. So, "luke" before you leap.

4. Right after lecture is also a good time to draw on *other sources of information*. Rechecking in the textbook and other books, through bull sessions, and the rest, may now turn up points you may not have noticed before. If so, jot them down while the subject is warm and before they slip away from you—I have found a pocket notebook useful for collecting such nuggets, or they can be entered directly in notes or textbook (see below). Do not worry about accumulating a tangle of memos: I am coming to that. But fill-in and round-out your notes while they are fresh.

Consolidating Your Material, One Method

Now, what do you do with your harvest, whether a conventional haystack or a select gleaning?

Conventional, exhaustive notes, used as an accessory or even primary text, cause time-wasting confusion. You have to straddle between them and the book continuously; and this, when one is under strain, can make the mind "seize up." Although alternative sources of information are desirable, such sources must be integrated. This is hard to do with voluminous notes, much easier with selective ones. But in any case:

1. *Consolidate* your notes with the textbook (see page 47, footnote) as follows: (a) Enter in the margins of the book all significant points *not included in the book;* (b) underline or otherwise mark (see page 47) points in the book that have been *emphasized by the lecturer;* and (c) draw a light, sloping line through book material omitted or lightly *dismissed by the lecturer* and of obviously minor interest to you. Next (d) compare *order of presentation* in notes and book. If you find the former order appeals to you more strongly, or suits your instructor's demands better, mark the revised order of topics in the book. You will then have all material in one neat package, text and notes supplementing each other, with redundancies and duplications eliminated. And you can file your notes away, probably forever—impious as this may seem.

This plan has worked for me and many others with great success. By actually focusing attention and work on the special points made by the lecturer, it helps you to play up to him—you are far more likely to give the guy back what he really said and thinks important. By eliminating duplication and superfluities, you save the time and effort of which you never have enough; yet you emphasize discrepancies. By making you think, the method helps you to learn, as mere transcription can never do. Consolidation forms an ideal introductory "bite-size" assignment in a topic (Chapter 10).

2. *Consolidate other material* similarly. (a) The interesting clipping or abstract related to your topic should not lose itself in a folder or drawer; it should be put in the book—not loose to flutter out and be a nuisance, but stuck or stapled in. (b) Quotes from books or journals can be entered, too; in a card file, they tend to get disorganized, unless you are more systematic than I am or have time to be; in the book, they are always at hand. (c) If you expect to employ large bodies of material from alternate or accessory sources, you can write simply; "See McClusky, p. 142." Consolidate.

3. But one caution: Do not let this method get out of hand. Marginal notes can easily become a mare's-nest of undecipherable confusion if you do not use system. Think: Put references at chapter ends; if additions to a particular page are going to be extensive or numerous, don't crowd them into scanty margins but write them on an interleaved (and stuck-in) page or simply stick in the original page of lecture notes—this should not happen often. As with any technique, using your head makes all the difference.

In Sum

You can convert all your wealth of lecture time from hypnotized stenography to effective learning.

Pre-reading is an absolute must.

By restricting your notes, you can see where your material should be supplemented by judicious questions and other means.

And you can save still more time by learning as you consolidate, and in later review of consolidated material.

In fact, your annotated textbook is an ideal basis for further effective study.

Thus, intelligent lecture attendance can be an effective first step in real learning. To break away from a tried-and-true procedure, especially if the herd clings to it, takes nerve; but it pays. Sailors of olden times feared to lose sight of land but coasted anxiously from landfall to landfall. When bolder spirits struck out to sea, they opened the whole earth to their profit. So can you, metaphorically.

Basic Equipment: Your Brain—
Its Care and Upkeep

In my student days, I always looked with suspicion on advice about personal hygiene. It was likely, I felt, to be of the puritanical persuasion that "if it's nasty, it's good for you." In those days, I may have been occasionally right; puritanism did linger on.

Today moralists have sought fresh fields for their assaults on human nature. Advancing science has learned so much about what really is (and is not) good for us that any literate person can afford to laugh at old wives' tales. Therefore, the following recommendations are scientific, not moralistic. They are strictly to increase your work productivity, which they may do by 50 per cent or more.

In Study Your Brain Is Your Basic Equipment

The mind, science knows, is dependent on the brain; and the brain is a bodily organ fundamentally like other organs. Also, it is dependent on the other organs for its well being.

Thus, the idea that you can "will" your mind to superhuman feats is truly an old wives' tale. In Kipling's immortal "If," he requires that you should:

> . . . force your heart and nerve and sinew
> To serve your turn long after they are gone
> And so hold on when there is nothing in you
> Except the Will that says to them, "Hold on!"

This is possibly true for "heart, and nerve, and sinew," up to a point; but if you forced them to a series of forty-mile marches on a cup of water and a handful of oatmeal a day, followed by a shot of drug at night, you would not expect them to serve your turn very long—much less to win an athletic event. Why, then, should you expect your supremely more delicate brain to perform under comparable conditions? You owe it the care you would give any fine machine on which your fate depended. Yet most students abuse it wantonly and stupidly.

Brain abuse is of two kinds: chronic and acute.

The *chronic abuser* is usually an overmotivated, overanxious drudge. He toils inefficiently for long hours every night, making up for lack of technique by volume of effort. He gets fair grades without gleam or spark, and turns out to be a good second- or third-rater through life. Yet often he *should* be a first-rater.

The *acute abuser* is usually an undisciplined fool. He fritters away most of the term and then tries to make up for it by a final week of all-night cramming. He either cracks up or gets by on skin-deep, rote memorization, which fails him within a week, and leaves him with shoddy foundations and habits. He condemns himself to lifelong futility.

First-raters have always learned how to treat their brains—and treat them well.

For effective study, perhaps more than for anything else in life, you must be in strict training. Your brain will respond more than any other organ to an intelligent regimen.

Sleep Comes First*

It is also rather controversial.

Different people, one often hears, have different needs for sleep. We are reminded of celebrities like Thomas Edison or Winston Churchill who worked with overpowering efficiency, seemingly for days on end, and who lived to a ripe old age. Most phenomenal examples, however, had the faculty, the facilities, and the habit of sleeping deeply for brief periods several times a day. If you can do that, it might work. Otherwise, do not try to pose as a phenomenon

---

* I will repeatedly discuss this topic, and some others, in the course of the book. I will do so not through carelessness but (1) because I feel these topics to be vital, and wish to drive them home to you, and (2) because I fear that a hurried reader may miss them if he skips this chapter.

when you are a plain human being. Taking less than eight or at least seven hours sleep in the twenty-four is either stupidity, or a subconscious pose, or panic due to overmotivation, or all three. It does not work: As a long-time examiner, I can accurately pick the papers, bad or not good enough, written in a nonsleep daze. And how about the dull drudgery preceding and the foggy knowledge following that exam?

Also true is the statement that different people have different sleep-wake rhythms: For example, I myself start fresh and early; reach a low point around noon, when I can profit by a brief nap if possible; improve towards 4 P.M.; remain at a high till eight or nine; and then taper off. Others are below par all morning, pick up during the afternoon, and are at a peak during a long evening even through to one or two o'clock the next morning. The problem is: How far are these rhythms really inborn and to what degree are they due to habit? Thus, a person may have developed a mere habit of staying up late for purposes of conviviality and/or study, and is *for that reason* below par in morning classes and examinations. If so, he is heavily penalizing himself.

Habit is often unreasonably precious to its practitioners, who resist giving it up. Yet nobody else but you yourself can discover what is really your rhythm except by long, complex, and not wholly reliable tests. *You,* however, can do a little research simply, easily, and with confidence in the results, if you are candid with yourself. Do you really do efficient work by sitting up till 2 A.M. or are you just pottering at your desk and deluding yourself that you are displaying commendable zeal? Try putting those extra two hours into sleep for a week and see whether your work does not more than gain in quality what it loses in quantity. And remember, you are not trying to show *me* (who could not care less) what your real rhythm may be. You are seeking a possible improvement in *your* performance.

"Oh but," I can hear the routine objection, "I have so *much* to do, and I have no other time to do it in." This is largely a delusion: Your work piles up because you are doing it badly and, so, have to do it over and over; the more it piles up, the worse you do it, and the longer you have to toil just to keep your nose above water. Then likely, you waste really good working time on weekends in an orgy of "catching up" on sleep. Which also does not work but only makes you feel stuffy.

To get out of the bog, you must use other tactics. In later chapters, I am going to outline a method of study that gets results in much less time and that simply cannot be carried on for long sessions—any more than you could sprint ten miles. But to practice this method, you have to be in training to start with. So, sincerely and honestly find what schedule really gives you peak efficiency. But whatever it is, it should include eight hours' sleep, however scheduled.

To finish this section, let me cite the classics again, and prick a bubble. Longfellow wrote, and is often piously quoted:

> The heights by great men won and kept
> Were not attained by sudden flight;
> For they, while their companions slept,
> Were toiling upwards in the night.

A beautiful moral picture and one that has inspired many misguided heroics.

A modern commentator, however, has capped this quotation more realistically:

> It may be true that sudden flight
> Does not conduce to heights of greatness,
> While toiling upwards in the night
> Has odds on less instructive lateness.
>
> But yet, how many names and powers
> The pinnacles of fame adorning,
> Got there by sleeping eight good hours
> And rising frisky in the morning.

Emphatically, the foundation for any really efficient mental performance is a clear and rested brain. By controlled test, it can accomplish more in two hours than a stale one can in four.

How to Regulate Sleep

Even agreeing that you need sleep, how to get it is a further problem. Practical considerations enter. Sleep schedule, up to a point, is a matter of habit: Men working on night shifts can soon more or less adapt to what seems an unnatural routine, especially if they impose regular hours on their inverted timetable. Even so, such people are rarely doing acute mental work. Similarly, if you have been in the habit of dragging along till 2 A.M., you can break that habit and substitute another more efficient for you. That is, supposing you are not sentimentally attached to the habit; you cannot break one that you subconsciously cling to.

Very often you will realize that you are balking the demands of your brain for sleep. In that case you need simply respond to the demands of nature, secure in the knowledge that you are doing the best thing for your work. (This is always supposing that you spend the waking hours efficiently.)

But you may have established a mere, but stubborn, habit that you cannot break all at once. Thus, if you are accustomed to staying up till 2 A.M., and attempt going to bed at 11 P.M., you are almost certain to lie awake—probably flattering yourself half-consciously: "See? I'm just naturally a night owl. He doesn't know what he's talking about when it comes to *me*." Which is not a fair trial.

Rather, you should taper it off. Try to get an extra hour per night for a week; then another; and finally, if you still are not getting a minimum seven hours' sleep, a third. Chances are that your weary brain will gladly accept the first, and the next, and the next, extra hours. Within a couple of weeks, you will be adjusted to your new schedule, going to sleep promptly at eleven or twelve, and waking refreshed and keen for morning classes. Then, and only then, are you in a position to judge whether you are, or are not, better off. In particular, you are in shape to try out the study method outlined later.

Various aids to sleep are often recommended: the hot bath, the relaxing book, the light exercise, the glass of hot milk, the mild sedative, or a combination of these (and other) resources. Use them only if you are prepared to continue using them and can budget the time. If you become dependent on them as crutches, you will miss them when you try to drop them.

Three practices do make sleep easier.

1. Reasonably strict regularity in bedtime, at least on working nights. In all such things, the body can be trained to a routine as you would train an animal; but it must be treated as a very stupid animal which is easily confused if its training is varied too much.*

* This applies to all other body habits too.

2. A schedule of work *and* recreation that leaves you properly tired (*not* exhausted, which may even keep you awake). You will find such a schedule mapped out in the course of this book.

3. A technique of mind relaxation through muscle relaxation has been developed by psychologists. The last is too complex to be described here but consists, in essentials, of focusing your mind on one muscle-group at a time, especially those of the eyes and mouth, and making them go limper and limper, sag, float, drift, lie like logs on the bed. If these things do not make you sleep, you should talk to your doctor.

Diet Can Be Treated More Briefly

Your body, and brain, are built of what you put into them. In many cases the wonder is that they work as well as they do, considering the low-grade material that is served them. But often they could be made to work a great deal better by treating them as kindly as such irreplaceable properties deserve. Service them at least as well as you would a high-priced car.

Poor food has two effects, the immediate and the insidious:

Immediate effect is of many sorts. How anyone can hope to study, much less take an examination, bloated with a heavy meal of stodgy food, suffering subtle indigestion from overspiced trash, or half hungry after a "cuppa-cawfee-anna-chonklit-bar," is beyond my understanding. The fact that you are used to them does not mean that such practices are good; Eskimos are used to living on blubber, but it has contributed to hold them to a low level of culture just the same. On the contrary, a meal well chosen both as to amount and composition can put you in a good frame of body and mind. This is worth a bit of reflection on your part.

Insidious, long-term effects can compound the effect of poor meals. One often hears the dictum that if you have a Normal American Diet, you are all right for your vitamin, mineral, and similar needs. Any real expert would raise an eyebrow at this: Normal American Diets, he knows, vary enormously in quality from home to home and from institution to institution: I have seen medical-school cafeterias (where one would expect professional standards) that would induce deficiency diseases in anyone who ate there regularly. Surveys show that even luxurious home diets can be deficient in humble essentials.

Furthermore, individual needs for any element of diet may vary five-, ten-, or even twenty-fold. Thus, in the days of sailing ships, the crews all lived on the same vitamin-C-free diet, and some men would die of scurvy long before others showed any signs of the disease. The same is true in civilian life as regards many factors, lack of which causes deficiency diseases. You have to be very badly deprived indeed to show recognizable, clinical signs of such diseases. But undoubtedly many people are suffering from low-grade dietary deficiencies of one or several sorts. All such conditions have an inevitable effect on mental performance.

What you *should* do makes a long story, and I promised to be brief. One can sum it up in a recommendation to stick to "live" foods: fresh, uncooked or lightly cooked fruits and vegetables,* fresh meats, whole-grain cereal products, fresh eggs, milk and other dairy products, and such. On the other hand, stay away from "dead" foods: heavy bakery products, preserved meats, starchy desserts, heavy sweets, coin-machine delicacies, and anything that has been overcooked. The live diet may be more expensive, but you need less of it to satisfy your appetite. And it assures a reasonable level of all necessary food and supplemental elements of diet.

Should you, even so, take "vitamin pills"? In view of the fact that many people, probably more than are suspected, have extra needs for one or another vitamin or mineral, possibly you should. This is particularly true in the Winter or if you are stuck in a situation where getting a "live" diet is difficult. If you follow the other advice in this chapter and are still below par and subject to infections, you might try some multivitamin-cum-mineral product for a month or so and see if it makes a difference. It cannot do you any harm; the hypervitaminoses (disorders caused by *too much* vitamin) that one hears of are due to huge, thousandfold, overdoses. At worst, you will waste a few dollars.

Exercise

This is the third major health need. Man is an organism not two-hundred generations removed from a savage hunter who lived a

---

* Professionally canned and frozen products are usually about as good as fresh, and may be better than "fresh" items that have been lying around for some time or have been overcooked.

constantly active life in grassland and forest. Two-hundred generations is a trifle in evolution, not enough to transform a population.
How, then, can this imperfectly denatured hunting animal expect to
sit hunched over a desk by the hour, day, month, and year, and
keep his physical organization functioning vigorously? Personally,
I certainly cannot, and feel the gears grinding after a week of
inaction. In spite of a disability that restricts choice, I find I have
to exercise at least half an hour daily to keep my mind clear. True,
many people seem to adapt to a life in which exercise is limited to
running for the bus or a little light housework; but people can
adapt to all kinds of diseased conditions, yet this does not make
such conditions good and desirable. Our concern here is with top
performance.

All exercise is not equally effective.

1. The more enjoyable it is, the more good it does you. Half an
hour heaving and hauling at some gym apparatus may be better
than nothing, but it is not so good as some sport of skill and
excitement, or even as a brisk walk or vigorous session in the
garden.

2. Exertion is not necessarily exercise; a day spent standing
behind a counter, or rushing about some institution, may leave you
exhausted but far from toned up. Proper exercise should make you
breathe hard and perspire gently, and leave you with a glow.

3. In the present case, exercise is a means, not an end, and
should be regulated accordingly. Most people who have gotten out
of condition set out to remedy this with a cave-man schedule that
leaves them stiff, drowsy, and yet overwrought. They would gain
greater benefit, and satisfaction, by building up, over weeks or
months, from a modest level to an adequate work-out. All this is
common sense—which is, unfortunately, not so common.

A well-chosen program of physical recreation can greatly en-
hance your efficiency. The emphasis here is on choice, the choice
that is *best for you* by inclination and results. Civilization *has*
modified evolution to the extent that many streamlined human
types now flourish who would have done poorly in a cave-man
world. This does not mean that such people no longer have
exacting bodies and are exempt from the need for physical activity;
it means only that they need not go in for weight-lifting, football,
and the like, which other people may really need. Here, an
insurance-company statistic is interesting: Of all occupations,

carpenters are significantly the longest lived; by which you should not necessarily infer that a basement carpenter shop is what you need, but simply that this sort of vigorous, yet not heavy, activity is most healthful. In your place as a student, you are not trying to build up bulging muscles (as in cheap magazine ads) but to keep your circulation, digestion, and other systems in top condition to serve your brain. Your choice of exercise should be guided accordingly.

A Few Minor Notes

How about *stimulants?* By this, I mean stimulants in the true sense, alcohol and nicotine being rather sedatives, especially for mental activity.

The main stimulant that concerns most people is *caffeine.* This occurs not only in coffee but also, in lesser amounts, in tea and most "pepper-upper" soft drinks. Caffeine is useful and practically harmless, if judiciously used; its disadvantages lie not in itself but in most people's lack of judgment. If used routinely in considerable amounts (the five-times-a-day cup of strong coffee), it soon loses its value as a stimulant. Rather it builds up something resembling a "withdrawal reaction", that is, more or less unpleasant symptoms when the drug is lacking. True, caffeine users still feel that they get a lift from it, but this lift is up from a trough (due to a drop in blood level of the drug) back to mere normal. It is not from normal to a temporary, but perhaps needed, burst of extra energy.

Often the use of stimulant drinks is just a conventional "break," a little (or often an inflated) spot of pleasure to lighten the working session; or one simply accepts coffee with a meal in the same way as one takes butter for his bread, as a matter of course. Which is no great harm, except that it deprives one of a really useful asset in times of emergency. A truly astute self-manager would find some less sheeplike form of "break," and hold his coffee (or whatnot) in reserve. But perhaps that is too much to ask?

One rather absurd, but often embarrassing, effect of such stimulants must be avoided: They are diuretics. Thus an unaccustomed extra cup of coffee or tea before an exam may indeed stimulate your mind, but it will also stimulate your kidneys even beyond the extra fluid intake; in fact, a caffeine pill can do the same. Thus you may spend the latter part of your examination in distracting discomfort, or may have to appeal for permission to absent yourself, which will not help your composure either. This one small tip may save you an exam, some day.

2. As for *"pep pills"* and the like, these are a fool's resource. I speak from practical, not moral, grounds. If used to flog the mind through a pre-exam endurance record, they will leave that mind drained for the examination itself—their stimulating effect cannot be prolonged indefinitely, and they will pile up a "fatigue debt." Applied to a series of examinations, this can be outrightly disastrous. If reserved for the examination, their effects cannot be forecast for any particular individual by even an experienced physician. In general, they produce an overexcited, flighty state of mind, far from the critical, sober judgment that produces best results, and more like the silly mood of intoxication. If you put your trust in them, you may rejoice in a reputation, among your confidants, for devilish daring, for what that is worth. But you will probably find yourself in a mess.

3. *Recreation* should, perhaps, be counted as a major need. "All work and no play makes Jack a dull boy" is not just an old-fashioned saying; scientific tests have proved very emphatically that any mental work is improved by periodically relaxing the mind. Of course, well-chosen exercise (see above) should have recreational aspects, so that this takes care of some relaxation. But that is hardly enough.

Relaxation should *relax*—take the mind completely away from the grind, or even from the exciting stress. Therefore, it should be suited to your personal needs and preferences. Some random amusement, taken up because it is handy, a casual book, television show, or chat, may be just what you need—or it may be a mind-wearying semi-bore. Of course, recreation should not be made a business if it is to relax you; but planning it can be profitable.

So books are your favorite resource? See to it that you have an adequate supply of your *favorite* kinds (not just one kind, which may not fit every mood). Twenty minutes browsing at some good paperback stall can set you up for a month.

So TV really does amuse you? But certainly not *all* TV. Know when the programs you like come on, and budget for them. Look through TV guides for fresh interests. If you prefer something mature, many areas are now served by university and similar stations. If you like escapism, do not be ashamed of it; *use* it. Use what you like. Relax!

If you like dating or parties, small or big, go for them. Presumably you are old enough to avoid a morning-after drag that undoes all the good.

And so on for shows, records, spectator sports, hikes, gabbing on the phone, hobbies, crafts, scores of things, or any combination of them.

How much? You be the judge—*if you judge*. I assume you are in the studying game to win. Too much fun sinks you; too little dulls you.

In Chapter 12, I recommend your budgeting a slice of time for extras. You might do well to stay inside that limit, once set. But within that limit, do not make a timetable for *all* your fun; goof off now and then on an impulse when you really feel the urge—it will do you more good than any other recreation.

In Sum

Your brain is a physical organ, and a very delicate one. It is not an abstract "something" that can be driven and abused with impunity. Like a fine racing car, it will serve you better, under stress, the better you maintain it.

The major needs of a brain that is to function at top efficiency are: adequate sleep, all-round good diet, and sufficient exercise to keep the whole supporting body in good tone. These things, however, should be means to an end, and be directed accordingly.

Stimulants, such as coffee or tea, are more effective if used judiciously. Stronger stimulants are certain to backfire.

Recreation, well chosen and in due measure, promotes top long-range performance.

A little attention to these prosaic matters can improve study and examination performance spectacularly.

PART II

Study Methods and Techniques

How Not to Study
(and Some Guideposts to Better Things)

If you have never observed good technique, you will be satisfied with bad. You may even be skeptical of first-rate method and of its success as being due only to unfair superiority of its practitioners, and "above your head." The methods used by you and by the "normal" 90 per cent of your associates, you feel, are inevitable and are even the best available—to you. Thus you resign yourself to an overwhelming waste of time, of satisfaction, and of achievement. But this attitude is a mistake: Any student, from the weakest to the best, can learn and profit from improved techniques and will find them not unattainable but usually simpler than standard methods. The greatest obstacle to adopting such techniques is often your devotion to bad habits; therefore you need to root out these habits. You can best do so by debunking them.

Bad study habits are usually pure rituals followed through faith or mental inertia. Several of the commonest are presented below, each one described for recognition, analyzed for its true nature, and followed by a practical alternative. Their futility, I hope, will be made apparent enough to banish them from your life. Then effective techniques can more easily take over.

Rag-Bag Program

The most effective way to spend study time is to tackle those topics that seem most urgent. Right? No.

The student sits down resigned or eager but full of good intentions. He has scheduled a two- or three-hour session of work, sure to achieve solid results. Of course, he has no definite idea of just what he *is* going to do; but he will settle that now. Scanning his desk, books, and mind, he decides that it is about time to start boning up for an approaching history test and, for variety, a bit of biology appeals to his current mood. In history, he feels a certain uneasiness about the French Revolution (though he has covered it twice already this term); in biology, his interest has been aroused by Mr. So-and-so's classes on the mammals (though this is a prodigious topic). So, let's go!

But even if carried out effectively, topics thus selected evade effective learning. They may be poorly chosen to build up a well-rounded picture of the subject, or even for examination purposes. (Questions asked an instructor before an examination almost always lack any sense of proportion or likelihood.) The key to mastering any subject is grasp of its pattern and systematic development of that pattern; after that, real priority weaknesses stand out clearly. By hit-and-miss study the student overworks some topics, neglects others, and fails to grasp vital relationships between topics. His misapplied time and effort gather only a rag-bag of information.

With this procedure, compare the method of organized scheduling outlined in Chapter 12.

Mass Assault

Having picked his assignment, our student buckles down to work. He has set himself a truly formidable task—two long chapters or several shorter ones. This, he feels, is really digging into things.

So he sits and reads. His understanding, not to say his retention, grows duller as the quarter-hours slip by. Occasionally he checks to see how many pages he has still to go, and he may be forced to admit that he will have to chop off one or both topics in the middle (thus further disorganizing them). He brightens up momentarily when he switches from history to biology, but not for long. No checks (beyond an occasional mental mumbling) to see if he is really learning anything and to fix it firmly. And such a mass of material passes under his eyes that even if he *were* learning it, his brain would play strange tricks with it.* Finally he closes the books with a virtuous feeling of having done and suffered enough to placate any jealous gods. And next day he may boast, "I read *fifty-three* pages last night!"†

But suppose that at the beginning of next evening's ordeal, our hero paused to ask himself, "What did I *learn* last night?" An honest conscience could not be put off by: "Why, the French Revolution and the mammals." It would insist, "Yes, you *exposed* yourself to them. But what do you *know now* that you didn't know at this time last night?" A strict stock-taking would reveal a residue mediocre at best: To a hazy picture of grievances, mobs, and shifting governments, gained from earlier skimmings of the French Revolution, he might have added a few more names and dates, not in any very clear relationship. For the mammals, he might have added some picturesque detail to Mr. So-and-so's clear analysis: "Huh, so all rodents aren't *really* rodents, eh? . . . Well, he didn't mention diaphragms as a distinguishing feature. One up for me!" But as he had not mastered Mr. So-and-so's plan, these details would only have added to his mental jumble. In sum, he would have a handful of random scraps, already fading, in return for his laborious two hours.

Contrast this with clearly defined, limited objectives, chosen for value and processed for permanent mastery, as discussed in Chapter 10.

Cross-References—Bogging and Scuttling

Any study worth the name entails looking up and clarifying unfamiliar or badly remembered points met in the course of the work. But the process can run to two extremes.

The student may read ahead hypnotically, growing more and more lost. He will check that baffling point when he gets to the end of the section, hoping that meantime it will all "come out in the

---

* Recent research has developed the concept of "information glut": The mind, swamped with new information, distorts it, oversimplifies it falsely, confuses it with something easy and familiar, or simply rejects it and builds up an aversion for it.

† I well know that some instructors assign great slabs of reading to their classes. But if their teaching methods are so unrealistic, your studying methods need not follow suit. You won't satisfy these people by obeying them; quite the contrary.

wash." On the other hand, he may break his line of thought for every trifle; which is particularly bad if he has a tendency to digress, so that one thing leads to another or his eye catches something irrelevant he feels he should know and would just like to check. In either case, he has no businesslike, well-considered policy.

Without such a policy, a student wavers between the two time-wasters. He may obstinately plough deeper and deeper into a bog, getting not even the paltry returns derived from ordinary plodding, and perhaps building up a mental block against the topic; or he may scuttle around like a rat in an unfamiliar maze, surveying a jumble of facts, disorganized and therefore quickly lost. Obviously, a sensible compromise must be followed.

The unit method of study (Chapter 10) practically enforces such a compromise. Focusing on a specific, limited topic requires that you tie-in essential relevant points from elsewhere; but the restriction of time prohibits rambling. You get the habit of asking yourself: "Do I understand what he's talking about without this point? Yes, I do, for present purposes. I can check the point later." or "No, I don't. I'll have to work it in now."*

In the latter case, an apparently obvious resource is often neglected: the index of the book. (Remember, a good index was given on page 7 as a quality of a good book, and it should be treated accordingly.) Make a routine of always looking in the index for references, rather than leafing inefficiently back and forth; if several index references are given for an item, learn how to check and discard irrelevant ones quickly. In these ways you can make cross-checking an asset rather than a distraction.

The Underlining Ritual

Pick up a used textbook, and the odds are good that you will find it copiously underlined.† The student, grinding ahead in a

---

* Of course, if your cross-reference proves to be itself a major problem, you may have to regroup your attack and treat it as a unit itself. Do not try to cram it into the original unit time or extend that time.

† I am well aware that a majority of schools today provide the textbooks; and that these must be returned immaculate at the end of the course. Hence the following discussion would seem to apply very little to high-school but only to college levels.

However, this procedure of supplying books seems to me most lamentable. Offsetting the usually minor savings on the cost of personally owned books, is a grave long-term loss: For anyone really interested in getting educated, his mass assault, has felt an uneasy conviction that he should be "doing something" besides simply reading; and he knows that everybody else underlines—so this must be a potent ritual. The fact that it *is* a ritual is shown by the painstaking way in which it is usually carried out—when a quick stroke down the side margin would serve as well to mark something notable. But reliance on such incantations is sadly misplaced.

Not that underlining is harmful in itself, beyond a moderate waste of time. Simply, it is futile and a substitute for techniques of real value though rather more demanding of thought and energy. It is futile because it evades getting down to real business; it is a sort of promissory note to your conscience: "Look, I'm picking out the real meat so I can concentrate on it—some other time." You are still just mass-assaulting with a feeble accessory, repeating material passively without effective organization. For a charm, you might as well carry a rabbit's foot.

Real annotation of a book is a very different thing. *Outlining,* bogus and genuine, will be discussed in a following section; but look for outlines in your first reading. Even pre-reading should be active and effective (see page 26). Is your topic subheaded? Fine! Number the headings, and *learn* them. If it lacks headings, this is perhaps even better: You work them out and write them in yourself, which forces you to analyze and mentally organize what you are reading; then, again, you *learn* them. Now you have the beginnings of a solid framework on which memory can call. Do you find a useful group of facts, say, causes of the French Revolution? Number them, and learn *them—now*. (A red ballpoint is best for all such work.) Do you find a key passage that seems to get to the core of things, so much so that you are willing to memorize it at least in summary? Summarize it and *learn* it *now—*

---

old textbooks should be a permanent reference, especially if he gets into difficulty (page 69). And this would be even more true if he had annotated them.

If I were planning ahead for a successful education, I would circumvent this well-meant charity. I would buy, if I could, or otherwise obtain, copies of my textbooks, however shabby and however much trouble they cost me. I would annotate them as described below. And I would keep them at hand for future reference till they became obsolete or I was sure I had no further use for the subject. In fact, I did just that with my own schoolbooks when I was a student.

Do this, even as a high-school student, and you will gain a great advantage over your more docile companions.

or if time forbids, set a later time for it in your schedule. Do you find paragraphs and pages of long-familiar platitudes or of introductory chat? Run a diagonal line through them so that you can skip them on review.

Sometimes I clarify an important but muddy passage by simply rewriting it; I break up a long, clumsy paragraph with paragraph signs, or a sentence with semicolons; or I try to express it in my own, simpler words. This process again makes you think and gives you a record of your results.

These are just a few suggestions which you can supplement or improve on. But they all present active, not passive, forms of treating your book.*

Nugget Hunting

This is related to underlining; the underliner usually picks out nuggets, not key points. A nugget, as I would define it, is a compact item that looks like good exam, or even real-life, material; thus medical freshmen prick up their ears at any clinical references in their basic sciences. With this preference, I am in sympathy; the object of most study should be application (in exam or life) and a foretaste of this application strongly helps to fix material in memory. But nuggets are only an aid to, not a method of, study.

Nuggets never impart real mastery of a subject. When overworked, nugget-hunting is the earmark of the student who wants to run before he can walk or, often, even crawl. Laymen are notoriously often depots of medical nuggets picked up from popular articles, TV, and such; and laymen are notoriously disastrous practitioners of amateur medicine. Some physicians, when one talks to them years after graduation, declare gruffly that they "have never had any use for nine-tenths of all that foundation stuff"— meaning that they too are simply accumulations of nuggets, though bigger ones, and do not know the rest well enough to use it. These are referred to unkindly as "cook-book" practitioners; very useful fellows to treat common complaints, but they do not appeal to me as guardians of my all-round health. The same applies to all vocations from car repair to atomic physics—and exams; nugget-

* Did you number these devices?

hunters are third-raters or less. Proper pre-exam nuggeting will be discussed in Chapter 13.

Mastery of a subject demands pattern; and a rational pattern often has to include "useless" material. True, this material should be kept to a minimum, but then it more than pays its way by setting the "practical" material in perspective for easier and surer memory—if you use the pattern intelligently. Nuggets, yes; but to clinch vital foundations and joints, not as a system of architecture.

The Tiger and the Tiger's Pup

This term is used to describe the extra and the extra-extra cheer after the conventional three. In studying, it represents a minor but often damaging folly.

The student has spent an exhausting evening of mass assault (or even of real learning). He has toiled manfully, yet he feels, probably with reason, that he has not accomplished as much as he would like. He must cram in a little bit more; and besides, he may have heard that "what you learn just before you go to sleep sticks with you." So he leafs through his book looking, probably, not for key points but for nuggets, settles on one and runs over it with blurred brain, feels that this is not good enough, looks for another, and so on. Till at last even his stupefied mind realizes that he is not getting anywhere.

This stunt results chiefly in useless extra fatigue. It preys most often on pre-examinees who, above all others, need to face their challenge fresh and sharp. Any scraps of information picked up are random, disorganized, and (due to fatigue) often badly chosen. The just-before-sleep maxim is scientifically true, but it entails three conditions: First, the material must be *learned,* not fumbled over by a stupefied mind; second, it should be something really *worth* learning; and third, it should be learned *immediately* before sleep. Tiger-hunting rarely fulfills any of these conditions. The half-hour wasted would be better spent in recharging your batteries with needed sleep. And usually, nothing is gained.

You can, however, apply the before-sleep technique effectively— as usual, by a little planning. In the course of your work pick out special items that you feel should fit the before-sleep period: not-too-exacting, clear-cut, significant units. Record them, say by listing them inside the cover of your textbook. Now, when you finish what you have planned to do in an evening's work, and if you still have energy, you can tackle one item of this list (*only one*). But you must feel really able to master it, not stupidly heroic; in fact, you should be able to play it back (page 95), not just mumble over it. Then, go straight to bed; do not ruin the effect by fooling around for half an hour. Or better, go through your bedtime routine, take the chosen unit to bed, and process it just before you switch out the light. In this way, you really may gain something.

Outlining

Like others of the foregoing procedures, this can be good or deplorable, according to quality. In a sense, it is a form of the pattern-building that is a cornerstone of good method. But as usually done, it is rather pattern-building in reverse.

A striking example of this is in my files. A student with whom I was on friendly terms showed me his outline based on a set of my lectures. It was a really beautiful piece of typing, subheaded and sub-subheaded, indented and footnoted. And since he had made two carbon copies, he gave me one at my request. But this copy, apparently so much more thorough than my own skeleton lecture notes, proved of little value to me. Beyond a certain point, it was too rigid, too detailed to be worth memorizing. It was utterly impractical.

This student, in my opinion, simply wasted energy on his beautiful outlines. First, he spent much time preparing them, time which resulted in practically no learning but only in superfluous preparation for learning. Then, he saddled himself with an unwieldy load which he could not possibly carry in his head—the only place where information is of any use—but only resulted in a blur, however much time he spent on the stuff. And finally he had added one more ingredient to the stew of his texts, notes, and sundries. True, he was in the upper quarter of the class; but, by general faculty opinion, he should have been in the upper tenth—a big difference when recommendations are called for. He probably held himself back by excessive outline busy-work.

In following chapters, we shall deal with effective outlines. Briefly, the main headings of an outline should be fixed in the mind like the Rock of Gibraltar; then the divisions of each part should be mastered; and so on down the line, *as far as is practical, useful, and portable in the memory.* Some headings, of small present interest, require little subheading but should be identified, placed in pattern, learned so as not to leave an uneasy blank, and dismissed; others will demand detailed organization of varying degree. A pre-set outline, like the one described above, ignores these differences in value, and tends to become an idealized scheme with all parts in equal detail. So, work from the top down, *learning* the outline as you build it, and stop wherever further detail is obviously superfluous. No outline should extend beyond the point where it is "mentally portable." Otherwise it is a wasteful, impractical sham.

In Sum

All these procedures are empty gestures. They disregard an obvious fact; that *the measure of study is the amount permanently learned.* They consume time and energy "covering" material passively with a minimum of achievement. The little they do teach is fragmentary, confused, poorly understood, and soon forgotten. Thus they discourage and bore the student, and may leave him with phobias for valuable subjects or for all study. Worst of all, they exclude effective methods. Yet they probably make up 90 per cent of study effort.

But each of these methods can be replaced by something better:

Random program should be replaced by organized schedule (Chapter 12).

Mass assault should be replaced by limited objectives, "study units" (Chapter 10).

Cross-referring should be restricted by restricted study-unit time.

Underlining and all such rituals should be replaced by organized annotation.

Nuggets should be treated as reinforcements, not as a system of architecture.

Tigers and tigers' pups should be replaced by preselected bedtime units.

And outlines should be built and learned from the top down, not all in one mass.

But even when using such improved techniques, one may be applying only disjointed tricks, like a football player who can tackle and pass but lacks any idea of organized play. We shall now discuss "organized play."

A Method of Study

So now to seek an organized method of study.

A "method," however effective, may sound arduous. In the short run, the method presented here does indeed require more effort *per hour* than sitting poring over books; but in the long run, it reaps far greater results for less total toil. And it has the satisfying stimulation of a smartly played game, compared to tossing a ball around aimlessly. Its benefits go to those who are not daunted by such a prospect.

Studying how to study is what you are going to do here. As already mentioned, this topic has been curiously neglected in the past. Either a standard, and rather mechanical, drill was imposed, or a student was assumed to know how to study by some inborn, natural instinct. Today, a good deal of formal and informal student counseling is practiced—of which I have done not a little. And a variety of books are available, though all, so far as I have seen, are either too theoretical or too vague. This middle section of this book is an attempt to provide a down-to-earth, practical method to guide a student who wants such guidance.

Later chapters will offer specific advice on particular aspects of study. This chapter offers some general advice that applies to all study.

Motivation, Its Nature and Forms

This is the mainspring of study. No matter how good one's techniques may be, they will achieve only half-results if motives are feeble. But are not motives more or less beyond one's control? Yes, somewhat, but less rather than more.

Say, you are not doing too well, or are doing well enough but without any real enjoyment. Take stock of your motives. Almost certainly, you have other reasons for your difficulties, but faulty motivation probably underlies those reasons; and well-adjusted motivation can powerfully promote vigorous, enjoyable success. After all, motive means "that which *moves* a person."

First you should realize that motives can be classified as long-, middle-, and short-term.

1. *A long-term motive* might be, say, a glowing ideal of being a doctor. This might be compounded of a sincere wish to help humanity, of scientific curiosity, of the lure of a doctor's varied and often exciting life, and of an image of oneself in a dramatic role. All very fine, but such far-off, shining goals tend to fade from sight; one plods through years of work that is often dull, sometimes seems remote from practical doctoring, and almost always holds the eyes down from distant peaks to the road at one's feet. Students of my acquaintance, with sincere dedication, still seem to find much of their studies a drudgery to be submitted to with, at best, resignation. As a professor of my college days said, "Lots of people want to be doctors, but they'd like to skip being medical students first." The same, of course, is true of any ideal: Long-term motivation is vital, but it is not enough.

2. *Middle-term motives* are usually less inspiring and idealistic but, oddly, are often more effective in driving one on. Such motives are: upcoming examinations, pride in one's work and standing, rewards (such as praise, prizes, or private celebrations) from others or oneself, and the satisfaction of putting another milestone successfully behind one. These things occur almost automatically in any scholastic career. But as motives they are usually rather fitful.

3. The greatest *short-term motive* is genuine interest in your work. This tends to be the keenest and most continuously effective, when utilized, yet the most commonly neglected. Students who take genuine pleasure in study are remarkably few nowadays; not that they ever were a majority, but the proportion seems to have decreased over the past generation. No doubt this decrease is largely due to the modern rat-race which increases pressure till

most serious study becomes an ordeal if not skillfully handled. Also, pleasure is often crushed by the increasing difficulty of many topics and inadequacy of presentation. And pleasure is increasingly easy to find elsewhere. At any rate, zest in study seems to be a modern rarity.

Two things may help to revive this motive for you: *First,* realize that dreariness comes from slack yet laborious effort, that effective work, however hard, is rather stimulating and challenging. You will find in these pages a guide to energetic, effective work. *Second,* everyone now and then catches a gleam of the fascination to be found in any subject when it is tackled intelligently. Bertrand Russell said, "Isn't it fun to know things?" But effective knowledge is more than fun, it is one of the most deeply satisfying values in life, in itself and for the command it gives over things. A fortunate and successful few enjoy this experience regularly. Anyone can belong to that group by simply growing up.

In this connection, I think of a welcoming speech to an incoming freshman class at a school where I was teaching: The dean congratulated the students on having achieved their ambition in getting this far. Then he said, "You have spent two years in premedical studies. Did you enjoy them or did you go through them impatiently, waiting to get to 'the real thing'? You are going to spend four years as a student working for your degree here. Are you going to really live them or always be despising them as compared to professional status later? Will the same be true of your internship and residency? And will you at last hang out your shingle thoroughly practiced in discontent and disillusion? If so, whatever your standing, you will have largely wasted eight or nine of the best years of your life. Learn to enjoy whatever you are doing *now.*" I think that speech struck home to a good many of those students.

Motivation, How to Cultivate It

So you find your motives, usually the long- and short-term types, are failing you. Here are some things you can do about it:

1. Recognize that *motives are your business* and nobody else's. The higher you climb the ladder, the more you will find that the educational apparatus is designed to give you what you want, but

not to coax you into wanting it.* If your desires are half-hearted, or too remote, the pressure of having to hold a place in the world may push you mechanically on. But top achievement, to say nothing of enjoyment and zest, are up to you.

2. You *can cultivate motives,* even short-term enjoyment. Root out childish resentments at having to do something that is not all fun and games, and analyze (and thus disarm) prejudices rooted in former experience. Try to find the fascination that many minds, no different from yours, see in the work; let the paragraphs below guide you to fresher interest. This is vitally important: Because if you cannot enjoy your work now, even the tough bits, you will find your bright, long-term goal disappointing, drab and toilsome, when you reach it. Believe it or not, enjoyment is largely a matter of practiced attitude.

3. *Seek fresh inspiration.* Has your ideal bogged down in a mass of petty detail? Are you like an explorer who cannot see the mountain-pass to a new world, because of jungle, swamp, and small hills? Then, metaphorically, take time out to climb a tall tree and see the horizon and the stars again. Once, as a student, I got a powerful stimulus to flagging interest by reading a biography of the Mayo brothers; and you should seek some such refreshment when vision grows dim—even some popular article or a chat can re-kindle you. One cannot maintain an inspiration all the time, and one may find it fading to apathy unless it has more than mere successful examinations and routine to feed it. A pause to revive your big motives is far from time wasted.

4. *Clear the tracks.* Many things, large or petty, are motive-blunters. In Part I of this book, we reviewed a number of these: stodgy books, poor teaching, sagging health, and others; and we discussed ways of dealing with them.

Mature self-management pays off not only in better detailed study but also in improving your underlying drive. In the preceding chapter we scanned laborious but unprofitable methods of study which can discourage the stoutest and most dedicated heart; and there, and in chapters to follow, we discuss how to quicken the tempo and multiply the rewards of work. The results of such reorganization can be a revival of short-term zest and a blazing up of ideals as if the fire were fed with dry tinder instead of wet twigs. Do not handicap your motives.

* See the anecdote that begins the Introduction.

Standards

I am not discussing these from a moral but from a practical point of view. The tempo of modern life continues to demand more and more from educated people and to promote skilled over unskilled labor. Yet education tends steadily toward bigger classes, computer-type examinations, less personal attention from teachers and, often, more hastily trained teachers. This situation throws more responsibility on the student.

Effective students are not parrots, whatever their circumstances. Our classes in this medical school are made up of students with varied premedical training. All these people have fulfilled the same requirements in course-hours and grades. Yet if one observes them, those from certain colleges perform, on the average, significantly better than those from others; but only on the average. Leaders in the class, future outstanding practitioners, may prove to come from the less notable sources. These are typically students who *set their own standards.*

As in other departments of effort, you must, in regard to standards, steer a middle course between two extremes.

On the one hand, you may have grown up in an atmosphere of what someone called "postgraduate kindergarten"—all extracurricular activities and watered-down courses. In that case, what you might feel was a supreme and heroic effort would be no more than mediocre by adult standards. You might just barely fulfill the requirements for entering a medical, law, engineering, or other professional school. But you would certainly find this a dubious triumph, landing you in deep water. Many a student is baffled by his first encounter with professional standards and drops out for no other reason. Yet he would have been quite capable of coping—if he had learned how to do it in time.

At the other extreme, the self-organizer sets himself impossibly high standards. However ambitious he may be, the fact remains that nobody has more than so many weeks, days, and hours in which to work (Chapter 12); and nobody can, even with the best techniques, crowd more than so much into each hour. Yet the inexperienced aspirant will set out as if he had unlimited time, and strive to master material in all its ramifications, by elaborate methods, and in minute detail. Such zeal is rather unrealistic in a working world. Its practitioners tend to become ineffectual pedants.

The thing to do, as in any real problem, is to seek counsel. Try to understand exactly what will be required of you in the profession or calling of your choice and in preparation for it. Talk to teachers, counselors, and especially anyone you know who is studying or has recently studied to qualify himself, and try to draw them out on this point. Try to get a look at examination papers and to scan textbooks you would be using up there. Try especially to find out from real practitioners what you would really be doing (in contrast to romantic, but ill-informed, daydreams) as a doctor, lawyer, engineer, or whatnot. Sometimes, one can get a little practical experience in a summer job, say as a hospital orderly or a factory worker. Then you can prepare yourself realistically for a real career, not fancifully for some fiction, glamorous or impossibly stern. Know clearly where your present efforts are leading. Then you can gear your standards to match.

The System

Based on these generalities, we shall proceed to particulars.

The following chapters contain what may seem like a good deal of advice. Do you really need to follow it all?

I will say this much: Each particular technique has proved useful to most of the students who have tried it fairly. And all such students have found 90 per cent (if not always quite the same 90) of the techniques useful. Thus, any one technique is likely to be of value to you separately, and several will be better than one. But isolated techniques lose power outside the over-all system, in which they support each other. The system *is* a system, not a collection of rules.

True, the exceptional unsatisfactory 10 per cent does occur. Certain procedures may turn out to be ineffective and irksome for your individual personality. If such is really the case, after fair trial and not because of whim and prejudice, by all means drop them. But do try them again after your program is under way; you may find that they look and perform differently in proper context.

The system is not as strenuous as it may look at first glance. When you are driving a car, an apparently unsurmountable hill ahead levels out as you approach it; and so will the apparent rigors of the system. In fact, once you have broken the grip of old, bad habits and established new, good ones, you will enjoy an ease of progress that you never dreamed possible. Getting into the swing of things is the only real difficulty.

This can and should be accomplished by degrees, not in one overambitious heroic effort. For example: Practice study-unit technique on one topic for a few days, then on two topics, then more, till it comes easily; then begin systematic reviewing; then try mental recall; and finally organize your programs. In this way you ease yourself pleasantly and naturally into the system. And it will never be a strain.*

The system does demand discipline. Restriction is necessary: First-rate work requires not only effort but organization, and organization means discipline. Mere earnest effort without method may be largely wasted as the untrained wrestler wastes much of his strength in clumsy bungling. Thus, if you wish to rise from mediocrity to excellence, or excellence to real mastery, make up your mind to tackle things maturely. That means, with disciplined system.

In Sum

Without *motives,* study is apathetic. Long-, middle-, and short-term motives are needed for full drive. You can cultivate them.

Without practical *standards,* study has no yardstick to check performance. Keep them in view.

With adequate motives and standards, you can follow a mature plan of study as developed in the following chapters.

Study itself will now be presented from three aspects: problem-solving (understanding), learning (memory), and application. Though problem-solving is difficult to teach, some basic techniques are suggested in Chapter 7. Learning is something that can almost

---

* Of course, if you are appealing to this book as a lifesaver just before some crucial test, you cannot "ease in." Even in that case, do not try to apply the whole system at once, but scan and pick out one or two techniques that seem to fit your case. Personally, I would take the study-unit technique (Chapter 10) and the short-term review (Chapter 11); and certainly I would take to heart the chapters on hygiene (Chapter 4) and pre-exam techniques (chapters 13 and 14) so far as these can be applied in the time available. Then I would read chapters 15 and 16 or 15 and 17, depending on the type of test expected.

always be greatly improved by the proper techniques, the best of which are summarized in chapters 8 and 9. Application, in your case, will be largely in examinations, but rehearsal too is an important form of application; so, Chapter 11 deals with reviews, leaving examinations to be discussed at length in Part III of the book. Efficient organization of time for all three purposes is discussed in Chapter 12. Thus, these chapters give you a comprehensive framework for study.

Solving Problems

A problem is anything that you cannot do and that you must do to fulfill your purpose. The unsolvable math or physics equation, the incomprehensible formula, the bewildering symbolism or jargon of many subjects, are the most obvious examples. But problems occur everywhere: the description of an event or process that you cannot make sense of; the statement "as a result of this" where you can see no connection; the piece of literature where you feel that the real point eludes you; the knotty piece of foreign translation. Often the situation seems to fit no pattern known to you.

Indeed, problem-solving is the hardest aspect of study to teach. Perhaps for this reason, all how-to-study books that I have seen disregard it. And indeed, one seems lost in a wilderness of difficulties, since every human mind meets problems to be solved for different reasons: lack of data, lack of experience, lack of confidence, lack of many things; and all these lacks differ in detail and degree. Nevertheless, some brief general advice can be offered.

Some Don'ts

Any problem can be aggravated by faulty treatment. Some problems can be irritated into mental blocks growing worse the harder you struggle. Therefore:

1. Don't be *intimidated or self-belittling*. The engineers have a proverb, allegedly handed down from our simian ancestors: "What one fool can do, another can." You are dealing only with school-work, and not with the unknown outer world. So consider that

many people, no brighter than you, have solved your problem successfully. Indeed, it would not likely be presented to you if it were beyond your level. Probably nothing more than some minor, temporary kink in your thinking is holding you back. Put your finger on that, and the problem will straighten out. You *can* do it if you go at it properly.

2. Don't get into a *mental squirrel cage*—running around and around the same cycle but getting nowhere. If the problem does not yield to direct, immediate attack repeated once or twice, it will not be likely to yield to the same attack made over and over. Yes, of course it *may*: On the third or fourth repetition you may spot some misunderstanding that is causing your difficulty. But the odds are strongly against such an outcome and in favor of your wasting time and developing a serious mental block. Better to marshal some of the methods outlined below, and attack from a different angle.

3. Don't, for any reason, *grapple obstinately* with a problem when you are *tired*. So you have a deadline on solving it? But you *will not* solve it by poring over it longer and longer with an ever wearier brain. You are very unlikely to come to disaster through failure to solve this one problem now (except on exams, and we are preparing you for those); and you are quite certain to be neglecting things you *could* do, and to be damaging things you *have* done by thus abusing your brain. Resolution is a resourceful virtue; obstinacy is a self-defeating vice. The following are a few resources.

Some Softening-up Techniques

Many a problem is a problem only because it is unclearly or unfamiliarly stated; or embedded in a mass of accessory detail; or a complex example of a simple class. Consider, then, how you can reform the material:

1. *Restate* the problem in your own words, the more bluntly the better. Ask yourself: "What's at the bottom of this?" (Calculus became much clearer to me one day when I realized that it was essentially a means of measuring curved areas.) Often a simple definition clears the air and solves the problem.

2. Express the *material* (not just the problem itself) in *plain*

language (page 145). A geometry theorem, for example, may be bewildering when expressed in formal symbols; "Bisect angle BAC (theorem II-I) and protract the line of bisection to intersect BC at D, etc., etc." But what's really going on? Why, you bisect this top angle, and the line looks as if it cuts the base in half; but these two triangles look similar, in fact they must be, so the base *is* bisected, and that's it! *Then* you can work out the points and dress it all up in symbols. (Sad, how many students plod through math, and other courses, without ever seeing the elementary processes behind the jargon.) Actually, this is the way many professionals work: Get the basic ideas intuitively first, and then formalize them.

3. Take a *simpler problem* of the same sort. As a childish example*, suppose you must find what 9/19 times 11/23 is, and have forgotten the rules for multiplying fractions. Well, 1/2 times 1/2 (or 1/2 *of* 1/2) is 1/4; and 1/2 of 1/3 is 1/6—you could even work this out by subdividing a square or a line. Obviously you multiply the lower figures. What about the upper figures? 1/5 of 2/5 should be twice as much as 1/5 of 1/5—2/25; 2/5 of 2/5, twice as much again—4/25. So evidently you multiply again. So 9/19 times 11/23 should be 99/437.

4. *Roughing out* answers is allied to the above. Thus in the example given, if you already suspect that you should multiply tops and bottoms, consider: 9/19 is almost 1/2 and so is 11/23; therefore the answer should be rather less than 1/2 times 1/2— 1/4; and 99/437 *is* rather less than 100/400 or 1/4.

Or, in another field, you find you cannot grasp a complex system of blood vessels; you lose one part of the picture as you grapple with another. So, draw a diagram showing only the ultimate basic components; master that and, perhaps, let it rest for a day. Then come back fresh and see if the details do not fit in smoothly.

5. Assume the answer and *work backwards*. In the triangle problem above, assume that the base *is* bisected.† This means the

---

* Examples used in this book will always be elementary; this does not mean they are addressed to elementary students. The examples are intended to illustrate methods of procedure, not as exercises or to convey knowledge. If advanced examples were used, say from my own field of neuroanatomy, they would be unclear to even advanced students in other fields. Therefore, focus on the method and disregard the simplified material.

† A classmate of mine once summed up this approach beautifully: "But doggone it! They *must* be equal or you wouldn't be asked to prove it."

two half-triangles are similar. But then, you can show this simi-
larity in other ways. And you've got it.

6. Break the problem into *steps:* Take the old puzzle of the man
pointing to a photo and saying, "Sisters and brothers I have none,
but that man's father is my father's son." Who is the man in the
photo? I have heard intelligent adults vainly argue this point in
circles. Now observe: That man's father is who? My father's son.
But my father's son must be I myself or my brother. But I have no
brothers. So that man's father is "I." So, he is my son. Simple—
when you do it like that; hard when you try to swallow the whole
rigamarole at a gulp.

True, finding the steps may be a problem in itself; but it is
usually a simpler problem than the original. Take a long-winded,
bewildering argument in a study of politics. Now (a) what is the
fellow trying to prove? *That* is usually obvious: say, that we can
easily support a much bigger population. Now, (b) what does this
mass of statistics show? That we have provided for rapidly growing population in the past (which proves nothing for the future).
Then (c) a quite different body of facts shows that we have
enormous, unrealized resources. Then (d) dismisses some counter-
arguments. Then (e) conclusion. Reduced to a, b, c, d, e like this
(and discarding b) the ponderous mass of writing begins to make
sense—or to reveal its fallacies. In short, you have reduced it to
simple steps—outlined it and thereby simplified it.

7. At least, *identify* the *fundamentals* (not quite the same as
roughing out). Say you are tackling the flow of blood through the
heart, in first aid; but you are tired and confused, and will get into
a squirrel cage if you persist. Still, you can pin down certain facts:
(a) The heart has two sides; (b) each side consists of an atrium
and a ventricle; (c) an atrium *receives* blood and passes it on to
the ventricle on the same side; (d) a ventricle pumps blood *out* of
the heart; (e) somehow, we have two circulations, one for the
body in general, and another for the lungs. Get those five facts
clear, and let the matter rest. Very often, your subconscious mind
will come up with an answer or a leading question. Thus the next
time you sit down to study, fresh, you are more likely to spot the
missing factor, say: (f) Each side of the heart receives blood from
one circulation, and pumps it out to the *other!* Then the problem
unravels. Getting the facts and waiting is a powerful, though not
infallible, technique.

8. *Compare* with similar problems met in the past. This should not be too hard in schoolwork, which is designed to build new activity on what has gone before; and where examinations are to test your ability in recent material. (In real life, finding comparisons may be harder, but train yourself now.) The deciding factor here is organization: Systematically organized material (see page 75) is far more useful here than is disorganized material. Thus, you may know all the examples individually, but grope around among them, missing the one you want, because you do not have them classified. You want your comparisons to be quick and thorough.

For example: In mathematics, you have studied series: 3, 7, 11, 15, where you simply add 4 (or whatever) to each successive number; or 4, 12, 36, 108, where you multiply by 3 (or whatever); and 4, 9, 16, 25, where you square numbers or raise them to other powers. Systematically apply these basic types (elementary, of course) plus any variants you have noted in exercises. You do not want to fish around like someone seeking a lost shoe in a muddy pond.

9. Set the problem in *context,* in the larger pattern of the subject. This technique usually comes first, instinctively, with systematic students—who therefore have fewer stubborn problems.

Thus, in the heart-circulation problem, much of the difficulty arises from isolating the topic. Draw back and look at the broad picture: What is circulation for? To bring oxygenated blood to the tissues. Hence we have one circulation to pump such blood to most of the body. But the oxygen must be continually replenished; hence we have a second circulation to pump deoxygenated blood to the area of renewal, the lungs. From this, one can *reason* out the organization of the heart. True, this requires a mental effort, which many people shun; but it is easier in the long run than trying to pound a lot of disconnected details into sense. Also, the results are more gratifying and permanent.

Setting-into-context can generally be done best by asking questions. How does this relate to what went before? Where is it leading? What is it for? If conditions were different, what would be the result? Is an alternative method or outcome possible? And so forth.

10. Finally, *intuition* enters into solving all but the most infantile problems. Intuition may be defined, for our purposes, as the

power to jump a gap, narrow or wide, between the known and the unknown. Suppose, in the case of mathematical series, you are given: 2, 5, 10, 19, 35, 69. You cannot fit this to any of the standard types, but know it *must* be a variant of them. You see that it mounts up fast like a multiplying (geometric) series—though it obviously is not; but it does not mount as fast as a squaring or cubing or other simple power series. Maybe a subconscious memory of some exercise, maybe just mental juggling, takes effect: Suddenly your brain clicks—those figures are suspiciously like 2, 4, 8, 16, 32, 64 and, yes, if you just add 0, 1, 2, 3, 4, 5, you've got it! You cannot quite analyze how you did it, but your mind jumped the gap. Some psychologist wittily called this "the ah-ha! reaction."

No one can formally teach or learn intuition. But, I believe, most if not all people start life with confident, natural intuition (as with confident, natural memory). They lose it by lack of confidence, and by reliance on mere plodding. So, take your intuition out of moth balls, use it on easy cases for a start, aided by the other techniques in this section, and build up your intuitive powers by positive feedback—success breeds success. If you can thus develop a power of jumping wide mental gaps with a good average of successes, you will have the most powerful problem-solving tool of any. All great problem-solvers have this quality; why not be good if not great?

These techniques, in various forms, will solve a majority of problems. But even methods 9 and 10 will fail when trouble is more deep-seated.

Are Your Sources at Fault?

Is your textbook unsatisfactory? Is your instructor dull or otherwise incompetent—at least for you? Are your own notes inadequate or full of errors? If problems are continually halting you, one or more of these handicaps may be to blame. A little thought may convince you that you are working with inadequate tools, and may suggest which tool should be replaced. The results can be surprising.

Summarizing advice discussed in Part I:

1. Shop around for a *better source,* one that is clearer, better organized, more suited to your tastes, or simply with a different

way of putting things. Two eyes give vision in depth, and so may two books (page 1).

2. Look for *popular* or *semipopular discussions* of the subject. These may put problems in a clearer light where they cease to be problems. I recently found, in a semipopular article, the key to a professional problem that had long baffled me—and which professional writers had *failed* to explain clearly. At least, such articles may kindle interest (page 5).

3. Take your problems to the *experts*. This should include your teacher himself (if he is not himself the prime source of confusion, or sometimes even if he is—often a poor classroom teacher can explain admirably to a single pupil); a proper teacher would rather spend time getting someone back on the tracks than in dull routine. But look for other advice too (page 9).

4. *Try integrating your notes and text.* This may clear up a jungle of confusion and bring into the open some point that the lecturer may have stressed, but the book does not, and that has been lost in the jungle. The critical comparison of notes and books, necessary for this procedure, often clarifies matters (page 30).

5. *Review your note-taking habits.* This may, at least, save you future trouble. As for hopelessly bad old notes, scan the notes of someone you respect (page 25).

These procedures may dry up a flood of unsolved problems. If not, you must ask yourself:

Is the Trouble with You?

Not: Are you a stupid incompetent? You would not be studying techniques to solve problems if you were. But: Are you an innocent victim of circumstances or a not-so-innocent victim of a misguided past? In brief, are you simply ill-equipped for what you are doing? This requires reflection.

1. Convince yourself that *this state of affairs must be set right*. To an already overworked student, the prospect of casting back, reviewing old material, may be appalling. Granted, such extra work is a hardship. But lack of it will certainly mean still greater hardship, even disastrous failure. The longer you procrastinate, the worse will be your trouble, and the less time you will have to solve it. A common medical tragedy is the patient who neglects a minor

disorder, hoping it will "just go away," till it becomes serious and perhaps fatal. Do not imitate such folly in your study troubles. Ignorance obviously won't "go away." And it is very unlikely to be cured by still more advanced work.

2. Clearly *identify your deficiency*. You can do this in two ways.

One, you can pinpoint your lacks, as you proceed with your studies: Are too many of the technical terms unfamiliar or uncertain in definition? Have you merely memorized formulas (or not even that) instead of grasping them? Do you lack basic vocabulary of a subject (say, a science) or of a language? Keep handy a pad, notebook page, or other record that you will not mislay, jot on it any terms that you need to master, and work on them till you know them. Do you have less definite, but disturbing, evidence that you misunderstand basic principles? Trace such faults in your foundations and mend them solidly.

Or two, you can scan through your old books on foundation subjects and discover what parts of them are unclear (page 47 note). Do not linger over muddles that really do not concern you at present—curious, how people who resist taking the time to mend foundations will go off on side issues once they have started. If you are having trouble with zoology, you may need to brush up on classification of animals, but not of plants just because you are weak on that too—not just now. Scanning foundations may take longer at the start than does mere listing of defects. But it can clear up difficulties more thoroughly.

3. To encourage you, you will probably find that *your defects are less than you might fear*. Often a very minor lack has thrown a widening shadow down a student's later studies, compounding difficulties; thus (I have found when tutoring people) a ten-minute review of basic *English* grammar can clear up many difficulties in the study of foreign languages; or proper grasp of a few elementary formulas can open up more advanced sciences beautifully. Then, too, you are older and more experienced than when you first took the earlier course. Or the very difficulties you are experiencing may cast a fresh light on former struggles. Quite likely, when you revisit old books, you will wonder why you ever found the material tough. And you will, I hope, be using the techniques advocated in this book, which also will help.

4. But if you find your foundations extensively weak, *seek*

advice. No student is so foolish as he who sits mum, nursing his troubles, hoping some miracle or superhuman effort will save him, when real help is within easy reach. Your teacher is there to teach, and this includes not only helping you to solve single problems but, much more, to evaluate your whole study situation. Many schools and colleges have appointed student counselors. (And you will find wisdom and experience at your disposal outside the school too, among relations and friends.) For example, few teachers, however gruff, will dismiss a well-timed, frank approach: "Mr. So-and-So, you know I'm having difficulties in your subject. I find it interesting, but the trouble is that my background is weak—I didn't have a very good course in such-and-such. But my time is pretty limited. What do you think I should do?" In this way, you may get not only advice but perhaps a certain leniency in current routines while you honestly try to pull yourself together. Don't waste time and energy struggling with a balky motor when you have skilled mechanics at your command. Don't let bashfulness, silly ideas about teacher hostility, or false pride stand in your way.

5. *Repeating a year* is the most radical means of dealing with a sea of problems. Usually this cure is imposed on a student— though I have seen cases where a student chose to repeat rather than build on shaky foundations. Even when compulsory, however, such a repeated year is by no means an unqualified disaster. Certainly, being set back a year, in this competitive world, is discouraging. But consider: The repeater was, in fact, a year behind already and has simply been forced to recognize it: for him to press forwards would be exactly like the fatal military blunder of leaving an effective enemy force in the rear; such an "advance" is almost certain to result in much greater disaster later when a longer investment of time and effort ends in failure, or when one faces the crises of real life only half prepared. On the other hand, I have often seen a repeater get a real grip on his work and carry on, thereafter, a step ahead of, rather than a step behind, the crowd. Such an opportunity can change one's whole life—for the better if one *uses* it instead of despairing or giving up.

A compromise with repeating, when one is in chronic difficulties, is the *summer course.* Say one has just passed a year by the skin of his teeth and realizes that he faces the next year badly prepared. One may not feel ready to sacrifice a whole year, but may well decide to devote a Summer to improving his position. The various sources of information discussed in Chapter 1 can guide one to means by which he can catch up with his competitors. If problems then become fewer and less formidable, such a Summer would be well spent indeed.

Practical means of solving problems, then, range from simple techniques up to radical revision of program.

In Sum

Problem-solving is difficult to teach. But it can be helped by special techniques:

Do not underestimate your ability, but do not try to solve really knotty problems by brute obstinacy or at an unfavorable time.

Soften up problems by:

1. Restatement of problem or
2. Of material,
3. Simpler analogs,
4. Roughing-out answers,
5. Working backwards,
6. Breaking into steps,
7. Identifying basic points,
8. Referring to previous, systematic cases,
9. Setting in wider pattern.
10. Intuition, an element in all problem-solving, cannot be formally learned; but it can be improved by exercise.

If problems are too frequent and/or persistent, question and rectify if necessary (a) the suitability of your study material and (b) the adequacy of your foundation knowledge.

Learning: Principles and Patterns

Learning is the backbone of study. True, to be effective, it must follow clear understanding; and to be of worth, it must be followed by application. But these two processes, in turn, depend absolutely on an adequate mental file of accurate, well-organized data. Thus, learning is of central, as well as extensive, importance for a student.

Unlike problem-solving, learning has accumulated a great mass of information about it. But the overwhelming bulk of this information is academic, of little practical use at present, or even controversial. Only a limited number of maxims apply to practical study.

A Favorable Climate for Learning

Effective learning is based on a well-directed mental attitude.

1. *A definite objective:* Your objective is *not* to "cover" material. It is *not* some far-off, hazy goal. It is *not* to avert exam failure by pious ritual. It *is,* and must always be, to *carry away now* clear-cut, permanent, lucid, usable knowledge—not just bushels of facts, but insights, ideas, techniques and, above all, basic patterns. Do that, and grades and satisfaction follow automatically.

2. *Confidence:* This is perhaps the most powerful asset to effective learning; whereas undue lack of it is a serious handicap.

Perfect confidence could mean almost perfect learning. A child who takes for granted that learning is natural, easy, and pleasant can rapidly learn an amazing amount accurately and permanently.* But as soon as companions, instructors, and others persuade him that learning is dull, hard, even a form of punishment, his unspoilt power vanishes. He acquires a conviction that memory is a matter of studious drudgery, or even develops a cynical lack of confidence in his ability (Chapter 14). Yet, I think, *any* memory is originally good, before confidence is shaken.

Wouldn't it be pleasant and profitable to recover this confidence? You can do so, at least in large part. If you find learning hard, you are probably suffering from a feedback: It is hard because you think it hard, which makes it harder, which proves to you that it is hard, and so on. The thing to do is to reverse the feedback: If you can achieve more efficient learning to even a small degree, you know it can be done, so you do more, and so on. Such a reversal may take some time, but it benefits you from the start and builds up momentum as you go.

3. *Exercise recall.* One direct way to improve confidence is: Do not be too easy on yourself. If you cannot recall something that you know you have learned carefully and with good technique, do not give up too quickly and run to the book; fight for it. Fighting does not mean forcing, fretting, and stewing, which often defeats its purpose. Rather, fish alertly for clues, associations, or memory aids (see below). Then, if this does not work, relax and go on to something else, but with the lost item held in the back of your mind. Just as with problem-solving, your subconscious mind may deliver the "lost" memory at an unexpected moment if you wait. This technique can be developed to a surprising degree.

It is of value on examinations. True, in such circumstances, you do not have unlimited time in which to let your subconscious work; but by then, I hope, you will have practiced the technique so that it works more reliably. We will enlarge on this when discussing exams.

4. *Effort:* Tests show that one retains best what he has learned with effort. This does not mean fruitless, inefficient struggle but energetic participation; the first is wearying and discouraging, the second, invigorating. Passive, stolid drudgery was analyzed in

---

*This is not the same as eidetic (photographic) memory, not uncommon in children, rare in adults. Eidetic memories are seldom insightful, organized, or well employed. One man displaying such a memory on a quiz show, to great profit, said that this was the first use his huge volume of remembered details had been to him. But quiz shows are not a way of life.

Chapter 5, and shown to be ineffectual through lack of organization; it is ineffectual also through lack of mental tone. This and following chapters will outline an active method of study which both organizes and stimulates. This is the effort of athletics, not of trudging through mud.

A degree even of physical tension helps—which may be why people knit their brows during mental struggle. Chapter 2 advocated a well-adjusted but not luxurious arrangement for one's place of study; one does not expect to study well cramped over an awkward desk *or* in an overstuffed armchair. People when tested showed improved learning scores when they were squeezing a rubber ball; one would do even better, I should think, with a firmly grasped, ready pen. Just as one must strike a happy medium between apathy and panic, so he must strike one between laxness and discomfort. Mental acuteness and physical alertness belong together.

5. *Interest:* Motivation has been discussed in Chapter 6 as the driving force for study, but it may be briefly reintroduced here as a direct factor in learning. Notoriously, one remembers best the things that arouse his personal interest—the exciting rather than the dull poem, the phone number of a fascinating girl rather than that of a boring one. You like and tend to remember a subject if you can see it as a valuable tool for your future ambitions—and hence interesting. Therefore, cultivate interest.

You may think that this sounds easier to say than to do. But you *can* do it to a considerable degree by well-directed effort. Assess your mental attitude: Is it mature and intelligent or based on half-conscious resentments and discontent? If the latter, determine to pull yourself together; read that section on motives again (page 54), refresh your long-term motivation, and seek short-term motivation for the matter in hand. Build up steam.

Maybe you feel the subject is forced on you by a badly organized curriculum—or that it is badly taught, or that you never liked that sort of thing anyway. So, are you going to let such considerations dominate you, causing you needless discomfort and costing you whatever value is in the subject? Remember that any subject is of fascinating interest to many people not too different from you; so it cannot be entirely arid. Since you have got to take it anyway, why not get some of that viewpoint? If you are weak in the general field, here is an opportunity to strengthen your weak suit by a little resolute effort. Again, seek better books, counsel, methods. As you progress, your learning climate will improve.

Which brings us to

6. *Success:* "Nothing succeeds like success" says the proverb. This may sound like lifting yourself by your own bootstraps; but it is an observable truth. The subjects in which you do well are those you enjoy—and vice versa. Doing well may be a matter of original temperament, or just of fortunate training; but the accompanying sweet taste of success again produces a feedback which enhances performance and further pleasure. And anyone of normal intelligence can succeed at least moderately in any standard subject. Success is the object of this book, and supremely of the following pages. But it should be courted not merely for its own sake but to heighten *interest,* spur *effort,* and build *confidence.* Then the whole system is a powerful interplay of feedbacks.

So much, then, for the general "climate" of learning. But other factors—soil, cultivation, pest eradication—are equally important in raising crops, and are more subject to control. In learning, similar factors are at work and will receive treatment in proportion.

The Foundation of Learning, Pattern

The key to effective learning is the mental habit of saying, not "I *will* learn this (I will, I will)!" but *"How* can I learn this efficiently and permanently?" We will survey various techniques, and even mere tricks, to suggest "how" you do this. But one principle underlies all of them: *pattern.*

What is pattern? This is difficult to say in nontechnical language. But for our purposes we may propose: Pattern is any arrangement of material that fits easily into our mental processes.*
Thus, the positions of eight dots scattered at random on a page are difficult to memorize; but two squares, of four dots each, print themselves on the mind promptly. On a higher level, prose with nothing to guide you but general ideas, rules of grammar, and chance oddities is hard to learn by heart; poetry (also with ideas, rules, and oddities) has measured lines, rhythms, and rhymes, and is comparatively easy to remember. (Hence, primitive, nonliterate

---

* I am aware that this is a rather circular definition. But so are any others I have seen. And it serves its purpose.

peoples memorize their legends in poetry.) So, the mind instinctively seeks pattern.

But not always very effectively. Most homemade patterns, deliberate or subconscious, are weak and faulty. True, even a poor pattern is better than none and may take hold after fewer repetitions than are needed for unpatterned material. Indeed, some patterns seem to catch on just because of their very absurdity, though this fact cannot be taken advantage of too often without resulting confusion. On the other hand, good patterns are hard to come by—indeed, *natural* good patterns are lacking in many topics. But the better and more vital a pattern is, the more effective it will be, and for more purposes. How, then, do you seek and utilize patterns in good learning?

1. *Proceed from general to more detailed patterns.* Always begin your attack on a subject with an over-all survey. Naturally, if you do not know the subject, you may be unable to tell what are the broad outlines, but you have certain resources for extracting them: Very often a good instructor begins his course with an outline of the material to be covered; a good textbook often gives the outline in an introductory chapter, and in almost any book a table of contents gives chapter headings and, sometimes, subheadings; an encyclopedia or similar source may give you a brief survey that you can organize into a pattern; "college outline" paperbacks are used by astute students not only to *re*view but to *pre*view. Personally, if I am going to study a book seriously, I learn the table of contents because this provides not only a framework for memory but a guide for finding things in the book. Later I may replace this crude pattern with something more logical.*

Do not learn the whole pattern with its sub- and sub-subheadings at once. Rather, first establish the over-all pattern and fix it indelibly in your mind. Then fill in each section *as you come to it,* with subpatterns, and learn *them;* and so on down the scale. (Compare this with the advice on outlines, page 51.) The more detailed your pattern becomes, the less exact your memorization

---

* An artist draws a human figure in just this way. He does not begin with the head, draw it in detail, then proceed to an arm, and so on. Instead, he sketches a "stick figure" showing the positions and lengths of body and limbs, the width and tilt of shoulders and pelvis, and other basic guides. Then he fills in masses of light and shade, and dashes for landmarks such as mouth, nose, and eyes. And only then does he begin to consider detail.

needs to be. In fact, you will find one great value of such a graded pattern is that it enables you to *reconstruct* many of the final details with a minimum of memorization. Thus, in a classification of vertebrates, having established the great classes (fish, reptiles, etc.) you can fill in many of the orders from common knowledge. So, the comparatively minor effort of learning main and subheadings pays for itself manyfold.

2. *Know the types of effective patterns:* These can be based, in order of importance and effectiveness, on: (a) logic, a reasonable sequence of facts, (b) generalizing or "packaging," so as to reduce a large number of facts to a few groups, (c) concrete association, a mental picture that is easier to call to mind than colorless abstractions, and (d) various minor devices discussed in the following chapter. Examples of a, b, and c (elementary as usual) follow.

For *logic,* observe the pattern of this book itself. This pattern may not be ideal, but it does attempt to follow a degree of logical plan: The three major sections are, in order of time, accessories first (you must have books and other equipment to study at all), then studying, and finally examinations. True, if you are following the advice in real life, you will probably adopt some of Part I, then of Part II, then back to I, and so on; but the essential logic remains. A similar arrangement is used for chapters in each part, as far as possible; and where this is not possible—objective-type exams do not necessarily follow subjective—you can twist things a little—objective exams *are* a later development in education practice; so "time" sequence still applies. Memorizing the table of contents by brute force would probably take you some time and leave a quickly fading impression. Memorizing by the pattern should take far less time and have a much higher recall factor.

Packaging is equally effective. Latin was a major subject in my high-school curriculum. As presented in the textbook, it was a formless mass of quite arbitrary rules. For example, the ablative form of nouns was used in a large number of specified places without any seeming connection, and caused me many errors in exercises and exams. Till, one day, a senior teacher pointed out that the ablative simply made an adverb out of a noun—telling how, why, when, and where; and thus, if you could simply recognize that a word or phrase was adverbial, you just used ablative and the heck with the rules. (You had one "package" rule, and a logical one.) After that, ablatives lost me few marks; even trick examples failed to throw me.

Concrete association is not quite so universally useful and, if forced, can be time-wasting and ineffective. But where it does apply, it is a very potent pattern-builder. For instance: In trigonometry the function called a sine can be defined mathematically with great precision, somewhat like this: "The sine of an angle is the ratio of the perpendicular from the radius vector to the base line." This is probably as clear, and meaningless, to most beginners as a Chinese ideogram; it is just there and must be accepted. But when it is to be applied to practical problems, the process would be a mechanical crank-turning, grinding out a poorly understood result, or would even be misapplied. After a while, if one had to use sines often, understanding might come intuitively.

But let me try to explain: The radius vector is like the hand of a clock moving backwards, from horizontal to vertical and then on past vertical to horizontal again. If a perpendicular line is dropped from the tip of this radius to the base-line, it will change as the angle between base line and radius changes: zero when the radius itself is horizontal, equal to the radius when this is vertical (and, so, equal to $1/1$), and then back to zero as the radius swings on. Fair enough: But of what possible use is such an abstraction?

Well, the sine appears in countless everyday and scientific situations. Take a concrete example; say you are trying to turn a crank: If you exert your push parallel to the crank—along it—you get zero turning effect; if you push at right angles to the crank, you get maximum effect, one full manpower (you cannot get more); if you push at intermediate angles, you get effects intermediate between zero and one. But these effects *are not proportional to the angle;* they increase at first slowly, then more rapidly, then more slowly again (though they are still increasing), as the angle steadily changes. They are, in fact, *proportional to the sine* of the angle.

Try some other examples: If you turn a page edge-on, parallel, to a beam of light, you get zero illumination from the beam; if you turn it at right angles, you get full illumination; and for intermediate angles, you get illumination proportional to the sines of the angles. So similarly for a sail, or a door, turned edge-on, at right angles, or at intermediate angles to the wind. So similarly for the force exerted by a crane working at various angles to the pull of gravity. And so on, and so on.

After a few such examples, the diagrams in the book take on new meaning for you: The sine measures a whole class of effects. Furthermore, you will quickly recognize that these effects all deal with rotation; you will have "packaged" the concrete examples. Then you can quickly recognize similar cases, even when the rotation is not immediately obvious: The slow change in hours of daylight at midwinter, the rapid change in spring, and the slower change at midsummer follow the sine law and depend on the rotation of the earth around the sun. And even subtler applications of the law can be made, as true understanding detects even less obvious rotations.

Thus, *concrete pictures* may promote learning (and indeed, help to solve problems). Abstract presentation, *as a beginning,* often fails to achieve such results. Its value is to *sum up* in a final package—as the sine, once you grasp it, enables you to measure many values quickly and accurately.

Observe that all these qualities of pattern more or less promote understanding. In general, the better you understand a subject, the better you remember it; and the measure of your understanding is how logical, compact, and concrete you can make the basic pattern. That is why some subjects are naturally easier to learn than others: They lend themselves better to logical, compact, concrete pattern-making.

Case History of a Learning Pattern

So important are these rules for learning that I am going to illustrate them further—again from personal experience.

In high school, we studied Roman history. History had always delighted me, and here was a novel realm of it to which I looked forwards with curiosity. But alas, our teacher simply began at the beginning and plodded ahead with no hint of pattern. The result was a mental scrap-heap of dates, wars, revolutions, constitutions, and men in togas or armor, unrelated and therefore largely meaningless and hard to remember. Even details that stayed in memory by force of drama rattled around loose in the chaos. The subject soon lost my interest and was hated by my classmates. Then, by disguised good luck, illness kept me home for some time, but threw me into the hands of a brilliant young tutor. Bill, after surveying my ignorance, began to build me a pattern, a sort of aerial survey of the subject: Roman history divides, broadly, into Republican and Imperial eras; the dividing line lies very nearly where B.C. passes over into A.D. *because* the first emperor, Augustus, ordered everyone home for a census, so that Jesus was born in Bethlehem, marking the year 1 A.D. (logic and a strong concrete association, you see).

Bill then broke the eras into periods. For B.C. we had: (a) a small city-state kingdom; (b) the primitive republic; (c) a long series of minor wars incorporating most of Italy into the Roman state; (d) resulting contact with Carthage, then the dominant Mediterranean power, and the series of Punic wars; (e) resulting rise of a formidable professional army with powerful generals who plunged the nation into a series of civil wars; and (f) the intervention of first Julius and then Augustus Caesar to restore order, resulting in the empire. (We need not bother with A.D. here.) But observe how Bill worked from over-all to secondary pattern, and the logic of his pattern: how one period *caused* the next, the disclosure of underlying tides of history. Observe also the concise packaging into six divisions. This has stuck with me ever since.

He then went on to give each period character. Men, battles, constitutions took their places in the pattern (learning by reconstruction, you see): The Roman fleet-building to defeat Carthage and the resulting expanded Roman horizon; the efforts of the Gracchi to deflect the course of disaster; how Marius's victories in Gaul paved the way for Julius Caesar; and so on. He thus shaped six-hundred years of history into a logical, fascinating and, therefore memorable, pattern.

The results were predictable. In spite of my apparent misfortune, when I returned to school I had a great advantage over my badly taught classmates in Roman history—and even in better-taught subjects that Bill still better organized for me. But I gained far more than this temporary lead: Bill had established for me a method of study that vastly improved my work thereafter and yet left me time for gaining a broader perspective. Such a *method* carries over into other subjects, as mere "mental exercise" does not. This legacy I here pass on to you as a major element of this book.

In Sum

You must deliberately set the stage for learning by adopting sound attitudes and policies:

Confidence is very helpful and can be cultivated.

Recall should be fought for to the limit, allowing the subconscious to act, before running to sources.

Effort (not struggle), even mild physical tension, benefits learning.

Interest, like confidence, can be cultivated and improves learning greatly.

Success is a self-promoting feedback from all these, and other, sources.

Pattern-finding is the essence of learning. It should:

Proceed from general to particular,

vary in form,

be logical, packaged, concrete where possible.

Learning: Aids, Tricks, and Fallacies

The systematic methods described in the preceding chapter are by far the most effective and rewarding. But unfortunately, some subjects can be tackled by these methods only in part, if at all. In such cases, one must have recourse to the rule that "a poor pattern is better than none."

Memory Aids

The following are some suggestions for, if not poor, at least more arbitrary, patterns.

1. A *standard set of subheadings* is obvious in such matters as biology. Here you can file facts about, say, each order of animals under such headings as: (a) place in classification, (b) typical members, (c) main distinguishing characteristics, (d) economic importance, (e) medical importance. And so on for other subjects. The essence of this technique is to fix your categories firmly in mind. Then, when called upon by examination or other claim, you have, not a confused mass of detail in which you can easily overlook vital items, but at least a series of memory compartments, thus: Order: monotremes, rather a low type of mammal; example, possum; and so on. When this process becomes habitual, it aids not only recall but also learning: It helps to focus attention on filling in the pattern.

2. *Number- and letter-sets* are commonly employed but can often be employed better. For some reason, many minds (by no means all) will remember rather easily that a certain group con-

tains, say, four or seven or whatnot, members. Having registered this fact, one has at least a check on recall: "Seven metals in this group, and I have only five; must find two more." This technique often works even better on long lists broken into patterned groups: "This artery has 18 branches, whew! But it runs through these four regions and, yes, in those regions it gives off 5, and 5, and 5, and—3 branches respectively." Even the irregularity at the end may help the pattern to stay in mind. Sometimes, similarly, twisting things to fit the pattern actually helps memory (effort, you see).

A further aid is grouping things otherwise than numerically. Thus, say you have 11 items to remember; but 3 have an initial A, 3 an M, 2 an R, and 3 miscellaneous. Or, of 5 names, 2 begin with Mac and 2 end in -son. This sounds like rather a feeble sort of aid but, the fact is, it often works in cases where you have nothing else to go by.

The real weakness of numbering, lettering, and the like, is that too many sets tend to produce confusion: Which set refers to which facts? Therefore, reserve the technique for special cases.

3. A *mnemonic* is a trick aid to memory—a rhyme, acrostic, pun, and so on. These are really powerful aids, when they are good; the trouble is that good ones are rare. In my student days, a drug company published a booklet of medical mnemonics, hoping thus to gain the good will of future doctors—and indeed, we received the offering with joy; but sad to say, few of the limericks, acrostics, or puns seemed to stick. As with number-sets too many bred confusion. Only a few old classics survive and aid successive generations of students. For example:

Pharmacists have an epigram: "-ate, I ate; -ide, I died," to remind them that cyan*ates* are harmless but cyan*ides* are deadly poison.

Medical students have an acrostic, of which the most respectable version is: "On old Olympus' towering top, a Finn and German viewed a hop," the initials of which correspond to those of a difficult series of nerves. Note that the silliness of this acrostic does not seem to impair its effectiveness.

Biochemists remember that: the *p*ituitary, *p*arathyroid, and *p*ancreatic islets secrete *p*rotein hormones.

Occasionally one hits on an original mnemonic, especially if one has "that sort of mind"; and one's own discoveries usually have a high recall factor. Thus, only the other day, I wanted to learn a group of anatomical structures named: supraclavicular, greater auricular, lesser occipital, and transverse cervical. My incurably trifling brain noted that these could be rearranged in a perfect jingle; can you see it? Anyhow, I am certain to retain the list where more serious students might fail.

But, I repeat, such windfalls are rare. And they usually cover only details out of broad and complex subjects. As far as they go, they may be received with gratitude. But they should not be sought with too great an expenditure of time.

4. *Word roots* again are only an occasional aid to memory; but they are very effective and scientific. In brief, most technical words are derived from Latin and Greek roots, recognition of which is desirable and easy.

Failure to recognize word roots continually amazes me. Students ascend through college to medical school, and even to graduate studies; but they never seem to wake up to the fact that the vocabulary of science is more than an arbitrary jargon of barbarous, tongue- and mind-twisting monstrosities. Hence they have to memorize, by brute force, hundreds and even thousands of technical terms, where a few-score roots would make the list a meaningful, and therefore easily remembered, system. Of course, a student must be impossibly dull not to recognize some roots through sheer repetition; one can hardly meet such words as hemorrhage, hemostat, hemoglobin, an(h)emia, polycythemia, and so on, without realizing that "hem" means blood. But he may fail to fit it together with the "poly" (many) and "cyt" (cell) in the last word, to derive "blood with many (probably excessive) blood cells." Yet such interpretation should be routine; it greatly aids memory.

A college course in Latin grammar is not needed to gain skill in root interpretation. Besides common roots learned by sheer insistence, as illustrated above, those given by thoughtful textbooks and instructors should be noted. Better still is habitual reference to a dictionary for the roots of unfamiliar words: Any good general dictionary gives roots for words in common use, and special dictionaries provide for technical vocabularies—medical, biological, philosophical, and so on. If you have not got the dictionary, note the words and look them up in the school library. This procedure may be rather a chore for a while, but rapidly eases up as you clear away the backlog of common words and need check only the occasional odd one; and it can become quite fascinating to the inquiring mind. Besides, it carries the solid satisfaction of increasing mastery while greatly decreasing labor: It means learning a short, easy, significant language rather than a long, difficult, meaningless word list. Make it a compulsive habit.

5. *Types of learner,* visual, aural, tactile (eye, ear, touch) are worth knowing about. If you draw a triangle with these types at the corners, most people can be placed somewhere near the middle; but many people tend towards, or away from, one angle, sometimes strongly. Thus, I myself am a poor aural, but a strong visual, and a fairly good tactile learner. This can be important to people with such biases: A tactile learner is bound to do poorly in conventional studies, and may rate as dull; but he may be highly talented in some field such as machine design or surgery. In view of my own bent, I never learned much from lectures till I adopted the methods described in Chapter 3. (I observe that good aural learners do even better with these methods.) Indeed, I got permission from some enlightened instructors to cut lectures on condition that I studied faithfully for the same period and got good marks, which I did. Similar realization of biases can, similarly, often turn them from liabilities to assets. Therefore, take thought on the matter—always recognizing that you are probably average.

6. *Memory systems* are mentioned here chiefly to warn you against them. Those I have seen are mere stunts of little practical value.

For instance, one method equates numbers with similar-appearing letters. Thus 8 looks like B and like (script) f. 2 (as Roman II) corresponds to N and H, and so on. Then, if you want to remember the street number, 82, of a sport shop, you relate it to the word FuN. But good examples are so hard to find that I have used the method successfully only for a few phone numbers.

Another "method" requires you to memorize 100 objects— apple, ball, cup, etc. Then, if you want to learn instantly another series of objects (say: boy, gun, cow, etc.), you pair them with your basic list in a series of fantastic pictures: William Tell's son with an apple on his head, a gun firing tennis balls, a cow drinking from a cup. This (not so easy) procedure can, I believe, be made to work as an impressive parlor trick.

But I cannot imagine these, or any similar, stunts being of use in practical study. Promises to develop an "infallible memory" lead only to your wasting money on a book, and time in discovering that the promise is a fraud. Would you really expect anything to replace intelligent effort in serious work?

7. *Flip cards* (also called flash decks and other names) are highly favored by some students; but they do not arouse my enthusiasm. These (to be sure you know what I mean) are packs of cards with, say, an English word or the name of a chemical on one side, and a foreign word or formula on the other. The owner of such a pack can thumb through it, guessing each answer and turning the card to check himself. This procedure would seem to be a good odd-time exercise.

But my reasons for non-enthusiasm are several: (a) Practitioners of this method have never impressed me with their grasp of the material even after much exercise. This is likely because (b) the method is an indolent one demanding little real thought or active participation—pattern-finding, packaging, and so on. And (c) the time spent on making a pack (or the money on buying one ready-made) seems equivalent to that spent on elaborate outlines or underlining; it is a "promissory" effort resulting in no learning at the time, and little real learning later. Thus, these cards do not fit the spirit of the methods advocated here.

Above all, this form of study excludes more fruitful methods. Spare-time mental review is more exacting and, for that very reason, much more effective. Wrestling with the foreign words or formulas, grouping them, packaging them, finding memory aids for them, can achieve much learning, and better learning, in the time taken to draw up the cards. Anyone launched on a program of real, intensive learning will soon look with impatience on such gimmicks.

8. *Programmed learning* is currently enjoying a great vogue. Questionnaires show students in many fields overwhelmingly (over 90 per cent) in favor of it. Indeed, I must admit, I am experimenting with it myself, just to keep abreast of things. But even so, I am skeptical.

This method seems to me a mechanical one. It may enjoy so much popularity for the very reason that it substitutes passive spoon-feeding for arduous thought. Yet in contrast to actively analyzing, comparing, cross-referring, reviewing, and so on, it would seem to provide only superficial, not critical, knowledge. As a means for imparting masses of raw material, it may prove to have merit. But, I feel, further organization of the material, and exercise, would be needed for any real grasp of a subject. At best, this method would seem to be only an accessory to effective study.

9. *Rapid reading* is a study aid the value of which varies widely according to the subject being studied.

It would obviously be useful where large amounts of material must be covered quickly and not too intensively: history, English, economics, and such. Though even in these fields, intensive study is necessary for some passages.

It would obviously be useless where much condensed detail has to be mastered: mathematics, chemistry, anatomy, and so on. Though even here, pre-reading can often be rapid, and some passages deserve no more than skimming.

Wherever used, rapid reading should be used properly. Those of its advocates whom I know, emphasize that rapidity should be accompanied by clear comprehension; they recommend learning how to seize highlights and by-pass superfluous detail and comment. Indeed, this counsel is very like what I give for short, condensed topics (Chapter 10): Get the meat, seek pattern as you go, attack the material actively—preferably with pencil in hand. Thus, a rapid-reading session would be simply a study unit for more diffuse material, and should be treated as such, with time limit, specific objective, title, and, above all, play-back. Rapid reading certainly harmonizes with the spirit of this book.

If you are lagging behind your classmates, find large reading assignments a chore, dread library research with its enforced scanning of many sources, are harassed by a piling-up of big and little things to be read, or cannot manage a fraction of the things you would really like to read—consider learning to read better, systematically.

Many colleges and even schools today give scientific courses in rapid reading. These can teach you to double your speed, if you are only an average reader—to double the amount that you can read in a given time, and read it better. Even a fairly good reader can improve significantly. If your school does not offer such a course, some near-by institution may do so, maybe in evening classes. If that won't work, well-organized books should be available at your library (see page 4), though a book of your own gives you fuller opportunity to master the method. In any case, a doubled capacity and improved efficiency, at least in certain subjects, is obviously a major triumph. Any effort, time, and expense involved are "setting a sprat to catch a whale."

Application

Everyone knows that you remember what you use. We will discuss how to use learned material in "play-back" during study, and in other ways, later. But anyone who devises active use for material learns faster than a mere book-grubber.

I have already mentioned the value of nuggets in nailing down information. Anyone studying for professional standing is wise if he refers to books he is going to use at later stages: surgical books for an anatomist; books on practical pharmacology for the novice grappling with basic chemistry; and so on. Of course, he gets value from them depending on how he uses them.

Too many people want to fly with pinfeathers. They would waste time, say, poring over the exciting details of operations rather than using a quick survey to vitalize and illustrate the mere anatomy that they have to master now. This sort of previewing can be a great source of entertainment and stimulation. But it should be treated as such and not allowed to intrude on budgeted study time.

Even better is practical experience. The budding engineer can transform his outlook by a summer's labor on some construction job. The medical candidate learns the hard facts of his profession as an orderly. Finance, commerce, law, politics, agriculture, and the rest, have menial jobs that will pay far more than financial returns. Such practical application depends largely on one's circumstances and determination; but in no case should it be allowed to exclude necessary groundwork. Beyond these comments, it lies outside our field of discussion.

In Sum

Useful accessory aids to study include:

A standard pattern imposed on each topic in any subject.

A habit of numbering, lettering, or otherwise tabulating material, to delimit what you have to know and break it into group patterns.

Mnemonics, a very potent aid when available, but not to be overdone.

Word roots systematically used to transform jargon into clear language.

More dubious or outrightly useless resources are:

So-called memory systems, which are no more than stunts of trivial value for real systematic work.

Memory cards, which are generally ineffective in proportion to time expended, and exclude better methods.

Programmed methods, which usually impart only packaged data without active analysis and critique.

Rapid-reading technique is extremely valuable in some subjects but of little use in others.

Applications, found by previewing work ahead, can be stimulating if not overdone.

Application through practical experience is ideal but depends on circumstances.

The Study Unit

This chapter is the core of the book. All that has preceded and all that will follow is certainly of value in itself; but when all is organized around the study unit, its value is multiplied, as when disconnected blocks form an arch around a keystone. The practice of study units is the advice I give to students when we have time for nothing more. Alone, this technique has saved scores and advanced hundreds of my students.

What Is a Study Unit?

I have already referred to units without defining them. What, then, are they?

A unit is a piece of work that you can efficiently and thoroughly master in one well-directed limited effort.

More informally, a unit could be called a "bite-sized chunk." It is an assignment that you can chew, swallow, and digest mentally without choking or indigestion. But note well that I mean *digest. Now.*

This demands several qualities for a unit:

1. It must be limited in content: I will, below, give and explain an arbitrary time limit of twenty minutes for a unit.

2. The material should fit into an over-all study plan: It should be part of a growing pattern, not an isolated "nugget" except in very special circumstances (pages 50, 125).

3. The unit should itself have pattern—or be subject to an

imposed pattern: It should not be a mere arbitrary hunk of material.

4. The material to be covered should be defined beforehand: "I am going to learn (or analyze, or solve, or whatever) *this,* and nothing more or less."

5. The best way to assure that a unit is a real unit is to seek a title for it: If you cannot give it a satisfactory title, you are probably dealing with "a mere hunk" and had better regroup.

6. Prepare to tackle your unit so as to master it *now.* No promissory notes (Chapter 5, In Sum). Expect to master it so that you will be able to give a solid account of it at the end of your twenty minutes.

An Example

All very well, but I pointed out in Chapter 8 that a concrete example may achieve more than any amount of definition. Let us, therefore, take our misguided student in Chapter 5, Mass Assault, and see how he might avail himself of unit study.

Our student has selected the mammals for one part of his evening's work. Since this would fill at least one, and likely several, chapters in any serious biology text, he is being pretty unrealistic. He could hardly cover such an assignment in the whole evening by the most superficial mass assault, much less master any of it. He has to focus down on something he *can* master in *twenty* minutes (Rule 1). He must select.

But now (Rule 2) has he got the mammals in perspective? Probably he has only the foggiest knowledge of the vertebrates in general, how the mammals differ from the other classes (aside from having mammary glands), what these differences mean, and so on. He might do well to raise his sights and take as his unit: "What *are* the mammals and why are they the highest animals?" He would here be making a step back in order to jump higher.

Suppose, however, that he does have the broad picture—by luck, or sheer repetition, or common knowledge. Now what? Should he take the first passage of reasonable length in the first chapter, and set to work? Not if he wants long-term results. Has he mastered a pattern for the mammals themselves (Rule 3)? Has he a clear, firm scaffolding that gives him confidence and to which he can relate new material? Almost certainly not.

Well, let us say he has a table of classification—subclasses, sections, orders—ready-made in the text. Fine! Now he knows where he's going: He's going to learn that table (Rule 4).

But wait. In his book, mammals present three subclasses, four sections of true mammals, and seventeen orders, all with crackjaw names, and many of them unfamiliar. Is he really going to master this catalog in twenty minutes? If his previous random work has broken the ground—maybe. Otherwise, he had better break the assignment into two "bite-sized chunks," each manageable in twenty minutes (back to Rule 1, you see). Let us say, he will take the major subdivisions—subclasses and sections—and since three of the sections are fairly small, he will also tackle the orders in those; he will leave the fourth section, which is bigger than the others combined, for a later unit. These two bite-sized chunks may seem almost too easy, but wait again.

Before he launches out, can he label his project clearly for present guidance and future reference (Rule 5)? The title need not be snappy; "Classification of Mammals, Stage 1" will do. And then, he should write it down some place.

All these preliminaries may sound rather cumbersome. Actually, they should take only a minute or two, and even less after a little experience. Once the over-all and secondary patterns are established, future units should practically prescribe themselves. The method is usually self-directing.

Rule 6, of course, requires more thought. However, the techniques are laid out in the summaries to Chapters 5 through 9, or in the chapters themselves if more detail is required. In the present case, certain recommendations would be particularly apt:

Pattern, natural or arbitrary, should be sought: *Why* are the mammals classified as they are? And can the names be grouped also by initials, acrostics, or other aids?

Roots of words would be invaluable: To realize that Chiroptera (bats) means "hand-wing" (and to relate "chir-" to chiropractor, chiropodist, etc.) turns the word from jargon to sense.

Traps abound. Unguiculates and ungulates are very different. Conies are *not* really rabbits, not even in the same section; manatees, seals, and porpoises, though all aquatic, are not related; and so on. Recognized traps become actual aids to memory.

We shall deal further with techniques below. But observe here how *active* study will fix material in the head, as passive reading, underlining, and such, never do.

Treated in this way, the two units will easily fill twenty minutes each. But now they will not require further time and yet further time in the future, but only brief, systematic refreshment (Chapter 11). They have been mastered, *now*.

Observe also that units can be of many sorts. The foregoing was an example of establishing basic pattern, and of almost pure learning. (This could well be done as a pre-reading assignment—see page 26.) In the same project (the mammals), one could also use units dealing with specific orders, fitted to a standard series of subheadings (page 82) and, again, learn the result. Often of very great value is learning a diagram till you can reproduce it accurately—a combination of packaging and concrete example. A diagram, as defined by one authority, is a drawing that you *can* carry away in your head without undue struggle. Such a diagram well learned is often of enormous value on examinations (see page 147). Or one could grapple with some problem such as comparing different types of limbs. Or one might carry out a review (Chapter 11), or search the whole pattern for weak spots (Chapter 13). In other subjects, techniques of problem-solving, or of application, or of grasping language rules, or of translation would predominate. Yet in every case, the rules given above apply: limited time, master plan, topic plan, defined objective, title, and "mastery now."

Following chapters will offer further variants of units and techniques. Just now, I wish to further emphasize some basic points.

Stick to Your Time Limit

You should not vary it more than a minute or two either way. This rule sounds arbitrary but is an important factor in your training. The famous Parkinson's Law states that: "Work expands to fill the time available for its completion." The reverse is also true: Cut down the time and the work still gets done, perhaps even better—within reasonable limits. Twenty minutes is a reasonable limit. This limit has several advantages:

1. It forces you to focus, to define your objectives.

2. It teaches you your powers and limitations. You learn to estimate closely just what you *can* accomplish in a given time and to avoid the lure of superhuman projects. This experience is invaluable on examinations and in later life.

3. Yet, limited time strongly promotes better performance. Working to a deadline, you soon discard bad habits: rambling, drifting, surrendering to distractions, and such.

4. The mind has a natural span of concentrated attention of about 15–25 minutes. Within this span, it can work at peak efficiency; beyond the span, it rapidly loses efficiency except in rare cases of great excitement. To break off and switch to play-back (see below, page 95) lets efficiency recover.

You may certainly use your judgment after a bit of experience. You may find that you work better in somewhat shorter or longer units (but not more than five minutes either way) at least for some subjects. If you really do get better results in this way, by *critical trial,* and are not following mere whim, you have my blessing. But having critically established a unit-time, do not change it except for serious reason.

Work Actively

Even a well-chosen and limited study unit will yield inferior results if you treat it by the mass-assault method (see pages 45–46). It must not be just read passively two or three times, or treated as a mere string of facts to be memorized. It will yield most, in the limited time, and will stick better if attacked actively, thus:

1. Keep always in mind the maxim: Not, I *will* remember this; but, *how* do I remember it?

2. Work always with pencil in hand.

3. Integrate as you go, with related units, to form a master pattern, and quickly check any points that raise questions (page 46). Tie in any outside facts that should help you to remember.

4. Annotate as discussed on page 48, noting subdivisions, vital words, names, numbers, and such.

5. Above all, look for internal pattern—pattern of any sort (Chapter 8). Maybe the mere subheadings will do; maybe you can spot a possible acrostic, pun, or other mnemonic trick, especially for names and dates—but do not waste undue time looking for

one.* Best of anything, look for reasons: "This naturally follows from such-and-such that I already know well, because . . ."

6. Finish off by focusing on the topic title and consciously linking it with the "how" of its remembrance.

Play the Unit Back

This is the feature most likely to be disregarded by the over-anxious student. Yet it is the most important step in learning permanently, for several reasons: (1) Awareness that a play-back is ahead greatly strengthens your attention, ingenuity, and penetration during the study period; (2) immediate play-back has been proved scientifically as the most powerful of all means to fasten material in memory; and (3) the play-back record faithfully shows errors and omissions in your knowledge. Furthermore, it is a constant rehearsal for examination, of tremendous value in the final showdown. Therefore:

1. Set a *definite length of time* for play-back immediately after studying the unit: say, ten minutes for a twenty-minute unit, and more, or less, in proportion to other units.

2. *Write* out what you have just learned, as if on an examination—of course without recourse to your books or papers. Mental muttering is not enough; it cannot be adequately checked. Do not scramble the presentation; make it as clear-cut, organized, and explicit as possible, as if you were writing an examination (see pages 144–149 for hints).

3. When you have done your best, then *check it* against your book. Have a special notation (say, a green ballpoint) for items in the book that you have missed or gotten wrong. Usually, when checked, these will have a high future recall factor; but some may prove stubborn, and you want to have these pinpointed to make sure you do not repeat the error. Give them special attention if you do.

Let me emphasize: Omission of this step is a glaring example of "more haste, less speed." You may "save" ten minutes by mumbling over the topic mentally as you grab for the next one; but you will pay tenfold and more by future laboring over the material, by

---

* If you do find one, you should record it. Most mnemonics are feeble, and fade out; but even a feeble mnemonic may stick, and help you, if you revive it once or twice. So, write it where you will see it again, in the text-book margin with your other notes.

inaccurate knowledge, and by loss of self-confidence. If the unit is the keystone of study, play-back is the cement that holds it in place.

Record Your Units

Keep a list of topics, with dates. This procedure serves both as a check on your systematic progress, and a resource when reviewing. A record staring you in the face is an admonition against a rambling schedule but is a solid satisfaction as you see your achievement progressing systematically and relentlessly. The techniques of using your topic list in review will be discussed on pages 104, 120. A good place to keep such a list is on the fly-leaf, or inside the cover, of your text—where you will not mislay it. Or title and date each topic in the book as you go. A profitable exercise, I find, is to recall your topics for the preceding six-or-so study days before beginning your new one for the evening. This you *can* do by rapid mental survey. You will discover that it gives you a gratifying sense of confidence.

Should you save your written play-backs? Maybe so if you have the desire, *and time,* to compare them with review efforts. In some cases, you may find such a comparison well worth while as an indication of progress; but for the most part, you will do better to concentrate on immediate performance and not clutter your workshop with dead papers. Certainly do not hoard them beyond the week-end review (Chapter 11).

Postscript: A Method for the Method

Study-unit technique, I readily grant, is exacting. For one thing, it requires self-discipline, and the trouble with that virtue is that it requires self-discipline to achieve. For another, it means real work: Three units, running about an hour and a half, will tire you more than three hours of passive exposure to material—as three sets of tennis will tire you more than an afternoon's rambling in the park. But if your objective is attainment, not relaxation, unit-work (like tennis) is far more effective—and exciting.

The natural objection arises: "But the book is five-hundred pages long! I'll *never* cover it in these 'bite-sized chunks.' " The natural reply is: "Will you *really* cover it by conventional methods?" Large parts of it must be skimmed in any case; by conventional methods you get hardly anything out of these parts and tend to skim the solid meat too; by unit study, you can extract the essence from many "dilute" pages and fit this into the over-all pattern. In any case, the method simply applies the same limited time more efficiently.

But it *is* exacting. Therefore, do not launch all at once on a full-time schedule, like the out-of-condition novice who tackles an afternoon of vigorous sport. Such a program is pretty sure to break down and discourage you. Rather, like an experienced athlete starting a new season, get into good form by reasonable degrees. Choose one subject, and do a unit on it every evening for a week; find out your limitations and abilities, the pitfalls you meet, the techniques you must improve; do not expect to master the method immediately, any more than you would swimming or banjo playing. Nevertheless, when you review at week's end (Chapter 11), the results are pretty sure to be gratifying. Then add another unit per evening, and then another. Develop the habit.*

A final application of unit study: You can use it at odd times. This is not the same as the spare-time mental reviewing discussed on page 102; it does require a solid half-hour under conditions where you can read carefully, play back, and check your unit. But if such half-hours are available, the procedure has not only the merit of employing otherwise waste time profitably, but also the advantage of isolating the units so that you are not overly fatigued and (I believe) recall them better than if they came in a bunch. For example, once when hampered by a time-consuming schedule, I needed also to cover a large amount of varied material; a session at lunchtime, one just before dinner, and one at bedtime did the job. True, this was far from ideal, and the schedule was ragged due to interruptions, occasional overriding fatigue, and so on; but it worked. However, I would not advocate trying odd-time unit study till you have thoroughly mastered the technique in regular sessions: You tend to get into slipshod performance unless the habit is thoroughly ingrained. And if you do use odd times, ease up on your regular evening sessions. Remember "information-glut" (page 46) and the need for refreshment (page 15).

* Of course, if you are using this book as a last-minute lifesaver (page 60, footnote) you cannot afford careful build-up. Even so, do not overdo things.

In Sum

A study unit is a "bite-sized chunk" to be mastered in twenty minutes.

The size of a "bite" may vary according to material, not the length of time taken to "chew" one.

Choose units carefully and systematically, not casually. Give them titles.

When working, do not stretch your time limit. Strictness improves performance.

Work your unit actively, seeking memory aids, pattern internal and external, and annotating your text so as to record your methods.

Immediately "play the unit back" *in writing*. This is a very potent aid to memory.

List your units and use the list as a basis for review.

The unit thus used is a powerful tool. But its power is enhanced further by a well-organized system of review.

Techniques of Reviewing

The time to learn something is when you know it.

This paradox means that when you have the first fresh, clear impression of a topic, you can review it and fix it permanently in your mind with least effort.

"But" you say, "I thought this study method was supposed to eliminate wasteful repetition."

No study method can eliminate review, but only *wasteful* review. Material, however simple, is rarely learned perfectly and permanently in one effort, even with the best techniques, and never (except by some freak) if it is difficult. By some quality of the brain, we seem to need at least two "learnings," with a fair interval between them, firmly to implant anything in our memories. Review, however, can be haphazard or efficient. We aim here to discuss efficient review.

How Review Economizes

One often hears cited a psychological "law": Material known thoroughly after one learning will fade predictably, leaving only 80 per cent after one day, and 30 per cent in the long run. One can experience this loss (I certainly do) after "mass-assault" learning, even if not in such precise terms; and the experience is often a great source of discouragement and dissatisfaction to students. But is so much loss really so inevitable? Can we not hope to minimize it?

Of course we can. Psychological tests are designed to measure memory in the abstract, not in real-life situations with many saving factors. In a typical psycho-research case, the test candidate learns a column of nonsense syllables or an arbitrary maze, an assignment with many differences from a practical study unit. The chief of these differences are interest, pattern, and review.

Interest (motivation) and *pattern* have already been discussed. They obviously create situations far removed from those of a psychology test. In the test, one's only motives are to beat the averages and to provide the good professor with valid data; pattern is deliberately excluded unless you can devise some acrostic or other stunt. Personal motives and significant pattern obviously should help you to better the 80 and 30 per cent showings.

Review, however, is the most easily controlled member of the trio. The only final proof that you really have acquired knowledge is to test your recall for completeness and accuracy. And the most powerful reinforcement of what you know, is to call out the knowledge—to convince your brain, so to speak, that you really intend to keep that knowledge on active file. You rarely bother to review nonsense-syllable lists between first learning and later recall; you have too much else to do and, besides, review here would be a sort of cheating. But in real-life study, you certainly do review material, which slightly or greatly improves the theoretical 80 or 30 per cent scores. Your aim is to achieve the maximum improvement.

Effective review employs definite techniques.

Review Must Be Active

Plodding through old material passively, even focusing on underlined highlights, is ineffective. It does not expose what you *think* you know, but in fact know only vaguely. And it does not reveal your inability to express what you know—indeed, if you cannot express it, you do not really know it at all. The one effective review, to check your faults and crystallize your knowledge, is play-back, preferably written but at least disciplined if mental. Hard work? Of course. But half-an-hour's hard work of this sort achieves more than an evening of lazy drudgery. Therefore, review by recall (usually written), not by a mere second (or third, or more) passive exposure to the material. Then check what you find to be delinquent.

Research confirms this advice. The more self-recitation (play-back) that testees use in proportion to mere reading, the more they retain, up to a point. Some enthusiasts recommend devoting as much as three-fourths of study time to such play-back. This seems excessive to me, especially if your reading includes annotation, organizing patterns, packaging, noting mnemonics, and so on; a 50/50 division would seem more realistic. And not all of your play-back needs to be at your study desk (see below).

Spaced Recall

This further promotes learning and minimizes drudgery—as opposed to effective effort. A systematic review schedule produces best results; good intentions and haphazard review soon degenerate into commonplace chaos and neglect. In general, intervals between recalls should be short at first, then increasingly long. A model schedule would be as follows:

1. Immediate play-back is incorporated in the study unit. This has been shown, again by tests, to be the most powerful of all reviews in establishing memory. It should on no account be omitted.

2. A quick review, at the next study session, before attacking new material, has already been advocated (Chapter 9). It should include at least a quick mental decision as to whether each topic is well in hand. If a topic seems delinquent, do not skim it but give it the full study-unit treatment; use judgment as to whether you do this immediately or as part of the week-end survey. This review establishes pattern as well as details.

3. Interim mental reviewing is discussed in full below.

4. So too, is the week-end review.

5. A major, over-all survey usually precedes an examination. This, accordingly, is discussed in the chapter on pre-examination techniques (Chapter 13).

Put all together, this sounds like a lot of reviewing, even a burden. It should not be. First, remember, it is a major element in effective study, as opposed to passive reading; and this attitude towards study must be developed in defiance of old, ineffective habits. Then, reviewing should never be allowed to grow cumbersome. When you have sufficiently reviewed something, by the methods described above and below, do not overdo the procedure —irregular flash backs undermine your confidence; trust your memory unless further study clearly shows that you have gaps in your foundations. Finally, your reviewing should be concise, efficient, "snappy"; in fact, at every stage it should be a rehearsal for examination techniques and for the demands of an active future career. Carried out in this way, every stage of review can be a stimulating challenge.

Mental Review

This is a valuable supplement to more formal efforts. Enough has been said about the supreme value of written work in unit playback and (below) in week-end reviewing, to establish its prime importance. Mental review, however, has its place between those milestones.

The essential thing, in such review, is that it must be well organized. It should never be allowed to degenerate into a superficial mumbling: "Well, of course, all that first part's obvious. Then there's that important business about such-and-such. And then hmha, maybe I'd better look the rest up some time—got to get ahead with that new material now." Thus you miss flaws in the "obvious" (and important) first part; maybe recall the easy (and not-so-important) second part; and look the rest up ineffectively at 2 A.M. the night before examination. In mental recall, pattern is supremely important: "Three main headings, which are. . . . All had four parts. . . ." and so on. You *know* when a piece of a pattern is missing; you pick around for clues (which intelligent study always tries to implant—*"How* do I remember?"); and if the missing item has not come to mind by the time you are ready to sit down at your desk, it will probably irritate you so much that you will check it at once. After which it will have a very high recall factor.

One beauty of mental recall is that you can carry it out in otherwise wasted time. How large a part of your day do you spend fruitlessly: on the bus, doing automatic chores, eating solitary meals, attending dull ceremonies, and so on? And how much of it is impossible to use for book-and-paper work for reasons of convenience, dignity, or such? This time is a great reservoir, supplementing regular study hours. True, to tap this reservoir, you need a special form of self-discipline. But (speaking from experience) one comes to cherish the habit.

"Yes but . . ." you say. You have already tried mental recall, and just could not make any progress with it. Probably not: You were working with vague, disorganized scraps that you could have recalled no better on paper. Now you are dealing with patterns and precise study units. Besides which, your effort was competing with the habitual wool-gathering in which we all indulge more or less and cling to as we do to any other bad habit. Some wool, if soft and pleasant, is good as a cushion between blocks of solid thought; but how much of it is downright unpleasant—needless worrying, brooding, irritation, or bored drifting in a "flight of ideas"? Learn to resent and reject such demoralization of your mind whenever it tries to take charge of you. Then combat it with well-patterned recall material, simple at first, already grounded in unit-study, and under favorable conditions; and work up to harder, longer assignments, even among distractions. Such profitable work is vastly more gratifying than the usual mental blur. And it is an effective way to undermine real problems (Chapter 7).

Filling *all* your time with study? On the contrary, by getting a large part of your job done in otherwise waste time, away from your desk, you can budget more time for real recreation and rest— far better than childish dramatizing, more refreshing than day-dreaming, fuming, and rambling. This is a habit that will make work and play more mature and satisfying all your life long.

A word about "overlearning" is in order here, because this is usually accomplished by mental review. Overlearning means frequent review of something that you already know well enough for easy recall, till you know it as well as you know, say, your fiancee's phone number, and will never forget it. ("The time to learn something is when you know it.") Overlearning is a good, not a bad, thing unless used indiscriminately: When a student has hundreds of topics to master, he obviously cannot, and should not, try to overlearn them all. The technique should be reserved for such basic things as major patterns (Chapter 8), vital tables, and such.

Week-end Reviews

For these, written work is mandatory. After a week's study, you have an accumulation of material, perhaps not very tidy because of stress and outside pressures; and you cannot handle this effectively by mental review. Furthermore, the human mind has a well-known tendency to subtly distort, and especially to oversimplify, learned patterns: thus, the 5-5-5-3 grouping mentioned on page 83 will slip into 5-3-5-3 or 5-5-5-5; and mental review will not detect such distortions. Thus, a quick *written* review is needed to pull things together and confirm true patterns.

However, this review should *not* be a laborious project consuming a whole afternoon or evening. As such, it would interfere with other activities and, very properly, tempt one to evade it and soon to get out of the habit. Rather, it should be a vigorous, keen effort to gain perspective on broad patterns, fill gaps, strengthen weak points, and correct misunderstandings; and it should take no more than an hour in ordinary circumstances. After which, other assignments and, emphatically, recreation should take over. As such, a review can be a source of satisfaction in cumulative accomplishment and final polish. It may be conducted as follows:

1. Your *check-list* of topics (page 96) is a good guide. Each day's work (I hope) has been roll-called mentally the following evening; now the whole week's list should be written out *from memory,* to eliminate errors and present the full pattern for visual inspection. The Friday, and even the Thursday, of the week just past can be omitted, as being too recent, and those of the preceding week substituted. If you have rehearsed properly, this should be an easy job. Now scrutinize the list.

2. Have you *forgotten* or *distorted* any titles? If so, you should probably mark them for further attention—though one *can* have a temporary blackout on a topic that comes back full and clear once its title is recalled.

3. Even if you remember them, do you feel that any topics are notably *unclear* in memory or contain *unresolved problems?* Mark them down too. If you have been working adequately, your blacklist should not be too long. Do not be underconfident; you have not time to rework the whole list. Then assign time to do unit studies on the delinquent topics—either at once or distributed through the week ahead.

4. Inspect the *pattern* of the work. Is it shaping up into something organic or is it just an aggregation of items? In the latter case, look for the underlying pattern—or devise one. Say you have been studying the Civil War: Can you divide it into periods, each

related to key figures and battles, and each logically leading into the next? Or is it simply a sequence of names and dates? Properly, you should have begun study of the subject with such a pattern, your instructor's or your own; but even so, are you keeping it in mind and fitting your assignments into it? Does it now seem good, or could you improve it?

5. Do you find any *significant gaps* in the pattern? Emphasize "significant": Has the instructor given weight to things that you have not adequately pinned down afterwards? Or do you yourself feel a void that leaves much unexplained? In the latter case, consider whether this void will probably be filled in due course during class; and if so, prepare to preread (Chapter 3) the material at the right time, but not now—unless very briefly to satisfy your curiosity. You undoubtedly have more than ample immediate material to keep you busy.

6. Finally, does your survey answer or raise *questions?* Your growing perspective may make things clear that were less so at close range. For example: The battle between the Merrimac and the Monitor was more than just a dramatic sea fight; it marked the last hopeful effort of the Confederacy to break the Union blockade. Or you may see that you have skimmed superficially over major problems: How great a role did that blockade play in deciding the war? Your examiner may expect you to answer such questions rather than display mere facts. This is a good time to anticipate him by thinking for yourself.

Altogether your week-end review should be more than a recitation of topics. It should be an occasion to make those topics significant. Significant material is remembered best, and is most usable.

One caution: Do not get overambitious and pyramid reviews of two, three, and more weeks as you go on. This procedure has several drawbacks: (a) It soon grows cumbersome and, as previously warned, discourages you from the week-end review entirely; (b) it overemphasizes earlier weeks, as these are reviewed again and again, oftener than more recent work; and (c) it weakens your vital confidence (page 72) in what you have learned quite adequately. Your pre-exam review (see page 120) should patch any real holes.

Of course, you should often scan the over-all pattern, the major headings past *and to come*. You should observe (with satisfaction) how this pattern fills out with illuminating details. But otherwise, concentrate on the job in hand.

To a beginner, systematic review (even if not cumbersome) may seem regimented, toilsome, even stuffy. It is the exact opposite. What can be more toilsome and stuffy than aimless, worried grubbing through disorganized masses of material, over and over, in the hope that some of it will stick? Or random, worried, ineffective flash backs? How much real leisure and pleasure, in and out of work, do these methods allow? In the armed forces, the literally regimented man is the enlisted man without the ability to achieve a commission or even noncommissioned rank; this man has to take orders because he lacks self-discipline. The man who has that discipline gives the orders and has the satisfactions of command, status, and opportunity, the more so the better the discipline. So too in any field of effort, especially study.

In Sum

Review is a major factor, up to 50 per cent of time, in any effective learning.

Review should be active, involving written recall, not passive rereading.

Review should be organized to give each item a series of recalls at increasing intervals—day, week, quarter.

Mental review cannot replace written but can be made a valuable accessory, utilizing waste time, if it is by pattern.

Week-end reviews should aim not only to fix material but to gain perspective.

Play-back, day-after, and pre-exam reviews are discussed elsewhere.

Programs: Big and Small

Having acquired the techniques of study and review, you can gain further substantial advantages by assembling them into an intelligent program.

Average students, say nine out of ten, have no program worth the name. They may roughly lay out an evening's work but then depart widely from even this hazy sketch. Their idea seems to be: "Well, after all, I'm getting the work done. I'll do all I can and quit when I can't do any more." By this method, or lack of method, one can waste a lot of time and effort.

The other one out of ten usually draws up meticulous, quite impractical, schedules. He then follows these for a while, with a glow of virtue; he finds himself forced progressively away from them by the natural stresses and conflicts of life. And he ends up in a tangle of frustration and self-disgust.

Only the very rare bird programs effectively; but he profits greatly. Teddy Roosevelt pointed out that routine is actually a release from petty details; it disposes of such nuisances automatically and efficiently; and it leaves the mind free for more important things. The good programmer realizes that his program should not be a strait jacket but an outfit for the game in progress. The following is one way in which he can outfit himself.

Programming (like motives) is of three ranges: long-, middle-, and short-term—say, for the semester, the week, and the evening. These types differ widely.*

* The three ranges of planning do not exactly match the three ranges of motivation (Chapter 6). Thus long-range motivation certainly should be

Long-term Programs

These should follow the Biblical maxim that anyone planning a building should first sit down and count up the cost.

Such an estimate would not take account of every stone and fixture. Yet study-programmers often do the equivalent of this: "I'll cover chapters 1 through 3 this week in six sessions, 4 and 5, which are longer, next week; 7, 8, and 9 the following week, and . . ." and so on for other subjects. Or they allocate things even more finely, earmarking sections for each evening.

This is quite impractical for two reasons: First, you have no real idea of how much time you will need for unstudied sections. True, you should preread (Chapter 3) and pre-outline (Chapter 8) for which the usual fussy planner probably makes no allowance; and thus you should have a general idea of what lies ahead. But you cannot foresee that Chapter 4 of your text will be brushed over as unimportant by your instructor (and therefore not be worth half a week), or that you will be hung up for several study units by Chapter 8. In the latter, more common, case, your fine program will be set back; and this, and further, setbacks will throw it into disorder. Then you will have either to reorganize completely or to pile on the work—both bad things.

For a second reason: Unless you are peculiarly well situated, you are going to have outside intrusions: family obligations, unforeseen chores, mandatory social events, term papers, two-day flus (if nothing worse), you-name-it. These too will throw your pretty program into disorder.

So, no long-term program? You might as well say, no estimate of building costs.

The prudent builder begins by asking himself not, "What do I need?" but "How much money have I, and how much can I apply to this job?" Substitute time for money: You have 90 days this

---

reinforced oftener than once a semester; and middle-term motivation can be relied on to assert itself as exams, and such, come up. Yet even middle-term motivation could profitably be refreshed at least once weekly by the satisfaction of seeing an effective program forging ahead on schedule. And short-term motivation, pleasure in work, could even more profitably be called on at the beginning of each study session: "Am I going to enjoy this effort, and if not, why not and what am I going to do about it?" Zest in work, I have said, can be cultivated, and this might be one way to do it.

quarter—say 75, to allow for those unforeseen setbacks and intrusions, and for essential recreation. How many study hours a day can you schedule? Let's say three an evening, which may be a bit heavy but will make our sample calculations easier. You may not always achieve this long a session, but week ends will raise the average. Then, say, you have six free periods a week during school hours, and two hours a day between classes and dinner-time—altogether about three hours a day. Do you want to spend all this time on studying, or part of it on recreation and relaxation—a work-out in the gym, or a stretch-out in an easychair, or just fooling around? So, say two hours out of the three for study if you think you can make it stick—and want to. Two plus three is five a day, times seventy-five days is 375; say 360 to be on the safe side again.

This looks like a lot of time—especially if you plan to practice mental review (page 102) in addition. But now, what must it cover? Say: biology, mathematics, chemistry, English, history, and civics. Six subjects, sixty hours each. But English and civics are snap courses; English is mostly just reading, and you can do that in spare time,* and civics is only a two-hour-a-week course. So let us cut formal study of English to 30 hours, and civics to 20. But math and chemistry are tough, with lots of exercises; so let us give chemistry the 30 extra hours from English, and math the 40 from civics. Biology and history are about average, so we will leave them at 60. That seems like a fair rough division.

But observe, it *is* a *rough* division. It is a line to hew to, but one that may need to be altered by later trimming and rearranging. Nevertheless, it puts things into perspective and proportion; it enables you to judge how you are progressing and applying your known resources.

Middle-Term Programs

These are for a week at a time. And first, how much time do you have per week?

A quarter is 13 weeks which, divided into 360 hours, is roughly

---

* *Can* you? *When?* In that easychair hour? OK if you say so. But the greatest illusion in study-budgeting is "sometime." Usually "some time" means "not at all," till you have to upset everything else to jam the material in, usually at the worst possible time. *Set* your time and stick to it.

28 hours a week. Allowing, as we have, over a day a week for interruptions, this roughly fits the four hours a day already calculated. And how are you going to apply this time?

The perfectionist will want to give each subject proportionate space. And this may be the best plan at ordinary times when you are simply forging ahead: three times as much for biology as for civics, half as much again for chemistry as for biology, and so on.

But often you will need to play things "by ear": How about that big examination in chemistry? Are you going to devote the full two preceding days to the subject? Will that be efficient? Wouldn't three hours a day all week be better? Then again, if you rob Peter (your other subjects) to pay Paul (chemistry), you will have to repay Peter and fit *that* into the *next* weekly schedule. And you will have to modify schedules to make up for time lost by illness, writing term papers, unexpected visits, and so on. Of course, you have allowed time for these things (15 days and hours) but see to it that they fit into that time, and do not crowd your basic work. Thus, many weeks will vary from the model plan.

The great thing is: *Know what you are doing.* Your long-term division of time between subjects plays an important part here. Say, after three weeks you know by referring to that program that you should have applied about fifteen study hours to history. But you have had to neglect it for reasons good or bad; now you are five hours short, and you should be aware of this and plan to make up the deficit systematically before matters get into a mess. Not that anyone needs to fuss about the odd half-hour or hour, but only to make sure that deficits do not pile up and create that mess. Such deficits make themselves felt heavily at the end of the quarter when several examinations find you badly in arrears in several subjects, with general reviewing to do. Periodic check on your progress prevents such scrambles.

Once set, how closely should you stick to a week's schedule? As closely as possible for the week's objectives which should guide each short-term evening plan. But, with your week's targets set, you should leave each evening's schedule to that evening and not try to plan in detail for a whole week. As with the long-term program, such detailed plans rarely work out and so lead to frustration.

Weekly planning time, however, *is* the occasion for criticizing your broad program. Is this working out as you hoped, or not?

Remember it was set up only on general principles, as a forecast; and it should be subject to revision in the light of experience. Maybe chemistry is not as hard as expected, because Mr. Blank's lectures make it so clear, and its time can be cut; whereas civics is tougher than reputed and should be given the time taken from chemistry. Maybe you have not allowed enough space for book reports; where are you going to get more? Adjust your program judiciously, always admitting that the adjustments themselves are experimental. But do not adjust on impulse, some evening, even if you feel it is justified; do it only after consideration, at the week's end.

One special tip greatly simplifies study-time book-keeping. If you do your studying at several times during the day, allot a particular subject for each spot. Then, casting back and forward, you can say, "Five hours a week for history before dinner is about right— 65 hours in 13 weeks. I did it last week, and the same for this." You can even put a particular subject in a particular spot in your evening's program, *if* you can be sure of a reasonably uninterrupted routine. In this way, studies will proceed automatically in proper proportion. You don't have to constantly bother about book-keeping.

Short-Term Programs

These are for individual study sessions.

If, as suggested above, you have particular subjects for particular times, part of your plan is ready-made. But only part, because you will have many special assignments to fit in, and will require to adjust your routines from time to time. Also, programs should respect certain rules.

We have observed (Chapter 5) the mass-assault program: A student sits down to a heavy slab of studying on one or two topics; he chews his way through his slab stolidly, or pokes around capriciously; and he ends up with mental indigestion and little nourishment. This is to a lesser degree true even of a crude series of study units. Effective learning requires more astute planning. As follows:

1. *Vary the menu:* You would not make a meal of a series of slices of baked ham, without bread, vegetables, or dessert, and expect to enjoy it or to feel fine after it. You have things to do

besides pure study: the evening program itself to lay out, reports and similar papers to prepare, reviews, special problems. You may have to make up deficits in certain subjects and go easy on others that you have favored for, say, exam purposes. All these things *must* be attended to sooner or later and will be easier and better done in short, effective stages than in long, dreary grinds. Even if you feel you have to put high priority on a subject, say, just before an exam, you will do better by spacing intense bursts of study on it with other activities. Avoid *surfeit,* the blunter of keenness.

2. *Place items effectively:* Planning your program comes first, naturally. Then: Are you a type that starts strong and tapers off, or do you build up as you go, or follow some other energy pattern? Order your menu accordingly. If a strong starter, do not let zeal of routine launch you on commonplace study units; tackle that forbidding problem first or in a spare period at school when you are at your peak. Save routine paper work for the end when you are tiring; or that might be a good time for your evening roll-call of topics (page 101)—if you can remember the list after an evening's work, you *really* know it. Reserve a preselected unit for a nightcap (page 50) *if* you have time and energy; but do not cram one in on principle. And so likewise if you belong to some other energy type.

Maybe you are having a dull evening when you are extra tired or out of sorts. Do not force your weekly program but use judgment. You might find this a good time for cleaning up small annoying study clutter—I do this with petty desk work on an off-color afternoon and feel I have used the time well. Don't flog a sick horse.

3. *Breaks are essential:* After an hour or so of really concentrated, active work, you need to relax the spring; even steel fatigues in time. To plod compulsively ahead soon dulls vigorous, active study. Budget a break after the first two or three items, something you can look forward to: a pleasant phone call, a cup of coffee, a brief easy-chair-and-book interlude, or just a stroll to the window to breathe the spring air. Do not wait till you begin to feel stale; you will find that prevention is better than cure for staleness. A second break, later, may need to be more vigorous, say a brisk walk or a hobby-shop interlude.

But don't let the tail wag the dog. You are taking a break to promote your study, not studying to earn a break. In this era of permissive indulgence (self and other) you have probably observed the type of student who "rewards" himself for a twenty-minute quiz with half an hour of gossip, cigarettes, and coffee in the hall. Judge for yourself if this is a mature, competent type.

4. *Do not duplicate units:* This may seem a trifle, compared to matters discussed above; but it is the ruin of much good work. By duplication, I mean a succession of two or more closely similar topics. For instance, our student in Chapter 10 would be foolish to follow his "Mammals, Part I," with Part II. Likewise, if you have studied the arteries of the leg, you must not now proceed with the nerves of the leg which are named and arranged in a similar but not identical fashion; or you must not follow a list of presidents with a list of secretaries of state. This procedure is practically certain to end in utter confusion with forgetting, after one day, of 70, not 20 per cent of material learned (another fact established by careful research confirming common experience). You should learn, review, and feel certain about those "Mammals I," arteries, or presidents before you touch "II," the nerves, or the secretaries.

True, you should, and probably will have to, compare the similar assignments eventually; in the present case, a doctor must know the relationships of vessels and nerves in a region. But this should not be done till both topics have been firmly and quite separately mastered with special care. Then, and only then, comparison will aid, not confuse, memory.

5. *Stick to your schedule:* Nothing is easier than to cut corners —or build them up: "Oh well, five minutes extra. I can stick them on at the end of the session. What's it matter?" This, believe me, can be the fatal spot of decay that will demoralize your whole program. The program relies on discipline, and discipline is exposed to precise measurement in an evening's program with its timed units; negligence here breeds disregard for other policies and a return to the old slipshod no-method. Just so, the driver who habitually indulges in minor traffic violations is a good candidate for real trouble. Watch it!

This applies especially to breaks. Since these are pleasant, stretching them is only natural and is hard to resist. To counteract this, rather than resorting to smug virtue, consider: Pleasure is always keener when it is rationed and loses savor when it overflows; the rich playboy who overamuses himself is notoriously bored, and the same is true on a small scale. Preserve the relish of your breaks by keeping them within bounds.

All this is not to say that you should be a martinet about the odd minute or so; absolute rigidity can be as demoralizing to constructive thinking as is laxity. Just do not let deficits creep up on you till they amount to a substantial total at the end of the session. Take pride in a smart performance.*

6. Nevertheless, *know when you are licked*. Traffic authorities speak of "highway hypnosis" whereby a driver carries on compulsively after his alertness and control are dulled; in fact, an outstanding feature of this dangerous state is obstinate persistence. "Desk hypnosis" is a very similar condition: One continues to leaf stupidly through the books and notes long after one has ceased to get anything out of them, just to stick to the program. A dull student may do this because he *is* dull; a bright student may tell himself, "Oh, I know. I'm not at my best, but with *my* brain I'll accomplish *some*thing by sticking to it"—but he accomplishes only fatigue and a blurring of material already learned.

This is especially true if you have been used to conventional, lazy study methods. You will find that unit-study is *work* which will accomplish maybe four times as much per hour but will tire you maybe twice as fast. Learn to recognize your cut-off point and not to waste time after it but to use the time better in recharging your batteries with sleep or real relaxation. So your program is thrown out of alignment? You will soon begin to set up more realistic programs. That is one objective of programming.

The Cost and the Return

You may spend half an hour or so planning your term, quarter, trimester, or whatnot; ten minutes a week setting objectives—about 2 hours in a thirteen-week block of work; maybe five minutes a night setting up a smart program—about 6 hours for seventy-five evenings: a total of 8 or 9 hours. Is this expenditure, out of 360 working hours, worthwhile? Even more, can you submit yourself to the resulting discipline? What do you get out of it?

* A prominent efficiency expert refers to accumulating small wastes of time as "slippage." Slippage gives little satisfaction and would sum up to a real recreation if used at the right time.

1. An efficiency that will probably pay back all the time by preventing duplication of effort, cramming, aimless drifting and indecision, neglect of one subject and overwork in another, and their kin.

2. A pride in your work that can carry you through rough spots with vigor and add valuable zest to your effort.

3. A justified feeling that you know where you are going, and measurable proof that you are going there. Nothing is better for morale.

4. An invaluable training for examinations (Chapter 15), and for your career beyond.

Winston Churchill remarked that if you do not keep on top of your work, it will get on top of you. To struggle under an undisciplined load is a miserable experience, however dedicated you may be. To crack the whip at your work is a source of power, enjoyment, pride and character. Try it.

In Sum

Without a program, work becomes sloppy; with too much program, brittle. A good program is vital equipment.

Long-term programs, for a trimester or such, provide a realistic matching of the available time and the work to be covered.

Middle-term programs, for a week, set goals and adjust them to progress and special needs.

Short-term programs, for an evening or day, set out immediate work efficiently. They should provide a varied, well-arranged menu with breaks and without "duplicate units." You should stick to them closely as you go, but cut them short if you have overplanned.

The results are well worthwhile.

PART III

Examinations: Approach and Procedure

Pre-exam Techniques

The week before a major examination, or series of examinations, is unique.

To most students, it is unique as a period of feverish delirium. All rules, all discipline, all horse sense are swept away in an orgy of sublime heroics. The well-drilled army breaks ranks, drops its modern weapons, and rushes on the foe in disorganized frenzy to come to grips with club, tomahawk, or bare hands. This is a tradition shared by everyone but a few eggheads—not all even of those; this is the magic formula for success, as the headlong cavalry charge against repeating rifles was the key to "victory" for the Sioux Indians. You're sunk if you don't follow it.

Or are you? Suppose, instead of stampeding, you unlimber and assemble your powerful weapons, assume effective battle formation, and advance according to a well-thought-out plan. You be the judge, after considering the plan.

Lay Out a Study Program

This is well worth more time than you usually apply to middle- and short-term programing.

1. As for all programs, *estimate your resources.* If you have been practicing unit study, you know about how much you can accomplish in a given time. And by the method given on page 108, you should know how much time you will have. Possibly you will

have a good deal of extra time due to suspended classes, which requires sensible handling. Do not get carried away by incipient panic or overambition.

Certainly, you are in for a supreme effort and must show how worthy you are. But worthiness does not consist only of grandiose overwork. Budget a little of that extra time (or of just your regular time) for breaks between shorter, vigorous efforts, which will keep those efforts fresh. Do not borrow time from sleep (pages 33, 50, and elsewhere) which is the major examination blunder that student counselors have to combat. But take whatever reasonable time you have and prepare to make the most of it.

How do you apply this time?

2. Whatever you do, *don't gobble*. This is a bad study habit peculiar to pre-exam week; it can delude even people following unit-study techniques. It is doubtless familiar to you! The wretched student sets out to cover vast, impractical sweeps of material (*not* the same as reviewing over-all pattern); he switches breathlessly from one topic to another, leaving each half-done; and he stretches this inefficient process later and later into successive nights as deadline approaches. The method is accompanied by a growing sense of tension, of frustration, and of boundless material still to be covered. Not very effective, you will agree; but inevitable unless you forestall it with a program.

The main cause of gobbling is a delusion that you have to review everything intensively. Faced squarely, this idea is quite absurd, since you could not cover a term's work thoroughly in seven days if you worked at peak efficiency for twenty-four hours a day. Your intensive work obviously should be very selective.

How, then, do you select?

3. Your first recourse is a *nonintensive review*.

Assuming that you have been building up an over-all pattern of your subject, by chapter, section, and subheadings (or otherwise) try writing it down *from memory*. Try to call up, as you go, the main points and memory aids of each heading. Make a real effort to get this outline full and complete before you check with book or notes.

If you have started systematic study only recently, and have no over-all pattern, make one now. Draw it up thoughtfully and revise it till you are satisfied. A "college outline" paperback may help in this case, though usually your own outline is preferable.

In either case, this pattern will lay before you, as nothing else can, your strong and weak points. Maybe you suffer from the conviction that you are weak all across the board and really do need to review everything. In the first place, this conviction is certainly more or less false. If you have worked on the material at all, you must have learned *some*thing and could present a fairly creditable account of many topics if you had to. And in the second place, you are assuredly weaker on some topics than on others. You will be better off if you pinpoint and *master* your weakest topics in descending order than if you make a head-on attack and give equal attention to weak and not-so-weak topics. Isn't that plain common sense?

This is why you should pause at each outline heading to recall basic points: If you can recall them only more or less, put down a red question mark; if you strike an almost complete blank, put down a cross; if you feel fairly safe, put down a check mark. Now you know where you stand.

However, strength and weakness are not the only factors to be considered. Importance of a topic must also be weighed: Maybe that topic, though vague to you, does not merit top priority. How can this be judged?

4. *Weighing of topic importance* should obviously be left mainly to plain common sense. If you cannot look at topics A and B, and decide that A, though unfamiliar, is far less likely to be used for test material than the somewhat less delinquent B, you are in pretty sad shape. But if, for some reason, you *are* in sad shape, or in cases of reasonable doubt, appeal to the following: (a) How does the topic weigh in textbook and notes? (b) Is it a key to much other material? (c) Is it a topic that seems to have great practical value for future studies or career? (d) Is it one that lends itself readily to good exam questions? In the latter case it is apt to tempt the examiner.

5. Your most neglected guide is, of course, *your instructor*. This seems so obvious that an inexperienced instructor expects to be mobbed by guidance-hungry students before every exam. Instead, he is almost ostracized during pre-exam week while bleary-eyed students cringe in corners and carry out exhausting ordeals of unorganized work. This situation, however, can operate in favor of the student who does consult his instructor. You can also *indirectly* get instructor guidance in two ways, one poor, one good.

Trying to outguess your instructor is an all-too-common but usually worthless practice. Students waste time that they would resolutely withhold from really profitable techniques, trying to judge the probability of a particular question's being asked: "He hasn't asked about such-and-such on the last two exams, therefore . . ." Such methods of crystal-gazing are thoroughly unreliable, even when your man often runs true to form. His least whim can nullify your guessing game.

On the other hand, pay intelligent attention to what an instructor-examiner says. Even if some board of examiners, not he himself, is to test you, he is a professional at gauging what is important, while you are more or less an amateur. Any competent instructor emphasizes what he considers important, not by length alone but by comment: "The key to this subject . . . ," "You will need to know this thoroughly when you come to . . . ," or outright, "This would make a good test question, wouldn't it?" Yet, as previously noted, I have myself made the last comment, only to reap an average of poor answers when I presented the question. Evidently, many class members were guided rather by, "He hasn't asked about . . . , etc." Hints are only a haphazard guide to study, but they are worth listening to when offered. So—listen.

7. On these, and perhaps other, grounds, *set up your program.* Write down your topics in order; don't just refer to your roughly annotated outline. A list has at least three advantages: One, nothing is so good for your morale as steadily scratching topics off that list, and observing your progress—*real* progress, not an endless attempt to gobble through a mountain of spaghetti. Two, your scratched-off list serves as a guide to review your review as you glance back at it from time to time for reassurance. And three, you can see that you are applying your efforts where they are most needed, not running around like a panic-stricken chump in a burning house, grabbing up ridiculous things and leaving essentials behind.* So, keep the list conspicuously in front of you.

If you like, you can earmark some special topics for immediate pre-exam study (see below). You should select these for value, of course, but also on grounds of straightforward clarity—material

* Many smart people keep a clear mental memo: "If the house caught fire I'd save the kids first of course, then the strongbox in my study, then get the car out of the garage, then grab my suits if I could or, if not, the family silver no insurance could replace. . . ." This is what your list does for you, and its visible presence keeps you from wandering.

that requires only simple learning, not brain-twisting. You do not want your brain in a knot when you sit down to that examination.

Now, Some Don'ts

1. Having set your program, *don't change it.* You should of course, do so for overriding reasons, such as some broad hint from your instructor. Even so, make any adjustments with care and caution. Remember, your judgment is likely to be worse as the deadline approaches than it was when you calmly laid down the program. Be sure any change is wise, not due to panic.

2. In any case, *don't stretch it.* If you lose time, or discover extra work, sacrifice the items at the bottom of your list. Loss of those items may be bad; an opening spiral of stress, scramble, fatigue, and disorganization is far worse. The temptation to yield to panic and cram more in is very natural; but it is a snare and a delusion. If, in addition to your groundwork, you give careful attention to a score or so of topics per subject in the week, you should be pretty solidly fixed. On the other hand you are not by stretching, going to cover more than a small fraction of the possible extra work, are going to blur what you already have learned, will break training and lose your keenness, and will shake your all-important morale. Tiger-hunting (page 50) is even more pernicious at this time than at others.

3. Don't *rush your topics,* especially with a view to packing more in. If they are worth doing, they are worth doing well enough to come out strong on an examination. What use are 50 per cent more topics if you cannot cash in on them in the final showdown? Give each topic full treatment as directed in Chapter 10.

4. *Don't,* in general, *tackle heavy problems* at this time. If you have been foolish enough to let such problems slide till near zero hour, you have two recourses: Either decide that you will have to pass them by philosophically in favor of more manageable, more extensive, and equally vital material; or if you are convinced that you must solve them, get help from an instructor, or other expert; the more expert your help, the better—two non-swimmers grappling in deep water may be worse off than one alone.

5. *Don't work in long heavy blocks.* Even more than in two- or three-hour evening assignments, you have got to guard against staleness and information-glut (page 46, footnote). Brief inter-

ludes between topics, and longer ones between groups, are mandatory. Make them really refreshing, not mere stodgy coffee-breaks. Have special little treats and rewards planned and ready (page 41). Presumably a healthy pressure will keep you from overdoing such relaxations.

Physical Condition

Everything said in Chapter 4 on personal hygiene has double force as examination time looms. The tendency, of course, is to slacken off, to cut down on sleep, on exercise, and on recreation, and to grab hasty, inadequate meals. This is less so for high-school students who are still somewhat under family control, and more so for college students who are enjoying, without experience, the satisfactions of independence. Odd how the undergraduate, who often has ambitions to set the world to rights, often cannot manage his own regimen efficiently. Indeed, he frequently persists in poor habits in the face of obvious bad results.

These results are familiar to every instructor. Run-of-the-mill depressed grades are too numerous to cope with; but, believe me, they are as numerous as the misguided self-punishers. The extreme case is unmistakable: In spite of flashes of obvious ability, his examination performance is ragged; he has misread or omitted questions, and answered others in erudite but confused style. His shortcomings are quite distinct from those of mere stupidity or negligent preparation. They give an impression of half-dazed competence.

Such a student, when he seeks or is asked to a conference, sounds like an overfamiliar record: "I don't understand it, sir. I was always in the top section of my class at high school" (or in lower grades). "But now . . . this exam looks pretty bad, doesn't it?"

He disregards the fact that he is now playing in a major league against the pick of many high schools or of several grades. After all, he started the year with satisfactory marks and has begun to sag only recently. An experienced counselor asks, "How much sleep did you get the night before that examination?"

"Well, uh, not very much, I guess."

"Yes. And how much sleep did you average for the week?"

"Well . . . four or five hours a night, I guess." (Probably nearer four.)

His other habits, when scrutinized, are often just as bad.

If he is then confronted with his paper and shown his short-comings, he is thunderstruck. He had not realized just how sub-standard his work was, even beyond the major omissions and misinterpretations he did remember. When writing that paper he was, in fact, like the drunk who thinks he is being wonderfully witty and fluent whereas he is only a bore. And our student was indeed drunk with fatigue, tension, and panic.

One then gives him what we used to call a pi-jaw—only it has nothing pious about it, just horse sense. Here, it can be summed up in one brief comment: You would not expect your body, or even a machine, to take outrageous abuse and then perform well on the day of a big trial. Whence, then comes the mystical notion that your brain can be "willed" into doing its best on an exam after a week-long punishing ordeal, of all times? Read Chapter 4 again and apply it firmly to examination week.

I refer you to the athlete: No first-rate player goes into a game, bout, or whatever, dulled with over-rehearsal and with lack of sleep, proper food, and mental relaxation. He, or his trainer, has planned in detail the twenty-four hours before the payoff. Now, the brain is even more sensitive than muscles, because its chemistry is even more delicate and precise than that of muscle. And it can perform no better than its physical condition allows, however hard you flog it. Will power cannot improve its performance; proper care can.

Every year, I save from one to half a dozen sleepless heroes by the same routine voice of experience. Catching short-order quick-lunch grabbers and washed-out desk athletes is harder, but they too contribute to lowered standards and dulled achievement. Catching people who do not fail outright but merely slip from what should be an 85 to a 77 standing or, which is worse, from a 95 to an 85, is even harder. One can only stress the obvious: Don't be a fool about your well-being.

Even so, many students are strangely obstinate in face of the results of their folly: *All* the sheep act likewise, so this *must* be the thing to do. Their only solution to difficulty is to indulge in drearier and drearier flogging, in a vicious circle of fatigue, poor results, and blind effort. Coax and threaten these zombies into a rational program and let them see their grades go up, and the brighter ones may be convinced. But I have tutored cases who were almost out of the woods due to a rational schedule, but who panicked and attempted all-night heroics before a crucial exam, and failed. In study, as in nature, the fittest survive, and common sense is a form of fitness. Use it!

"Just Before the Battle, Mother"

Now you come to the last twelve hours before examination. How do you use them?

1. Again I repeat: *A good sleep* is the top priority essential. I do not care how much material you do not (or feel you do not) know. A few hours' extra inefficient work are not going to be more than a drop in the bucket anyway; and above all at this vital time, they can knock down the value of hundreds of hours' earlier effort. Conversely, a sound sleep can set up the value of everything you do know. If I could give only one bit of advice to all examination candidates, strong or weak, it would be: "Get a full night's sleep."

You may have trouble going to sleep and staying there. Such trouble should be minor for those who apply this book; still, it bothers the best of us at times. If so, *don't experiment now.* You should know from experience what a brisk walk, a mild sedative, a warm drink, and so on, will do towards sound sleep and fresh awakening. Stick to experience.

2. A *morning mental warm-up* has been shown by research to be valuable. If you have enjoyed a full night's sleep, you can profitably get up a bit early and do some work. However, the nature of such work is vital: This is *not* the time to grapple with some extra tough topic, or to leaf breathlessly from one topic to another. Rather, you should calmly scan a couple of important topics with which you are fairly but still not confidently familiar, chosen earlier. This choice gets useful work done without straining your mind or shaking your confidence. You may think of football players just before a game: They do not practice heavy exercises or tackling, but run around the gridiron making passes and kicks, for their warm-up.

3. A *well-thought-out program* is practically and psychologically a must. It should include (a) a good, tasty, sustaining but not clogging breakfast, with time to eat it like a civilized human being;

(b) enough physical exertion to get your circulation going, such as a brisk walk; (c) a check to make sure you have all needed equipment, especially a full pen or ballpoint; (d) a fair but not excessive margin of safety so that you need not get in a lather if you are delayed but won't get in a stew if you arrive early. In the latter case (e) have a *pre-arranged* choice of light but worthwhile work to keep your mind occupied; don't mill around with the jittery, disorganized crowd.

Don't experiment with stimulants, even an extra cup of coffee. In your state of (normal) tension, these can backfire badly. Stick to your usual coffee, or other, routine.

Much the same applies to a later exam, usually after a morning exam and lunch. Use your head, plan, and stick to it. Further:

4. Have a *sustaining but not stodgy lunch*. This is no time to be economical. Stick to protein (meat, cheese, eggs, fish) and light sweets (fruit, good candy and cakes) rather than a lot of fat and starch. A famous test-pilot always uses chicken sandwiches with plenty of chicken, and chocolate, for long runs; a friend of mine did well on a good hamburger (with double meat, not too much seasoning, and an unsoggy bun) and an ice-cream soda. Anyway, stay away from cafeteria macaroni-casserole followed by doughy pie, or vending-machine sandwiches, all cheap bread and minimum filler, or nice, thick, homemade jam sandwiches. At the other extreme, don't try to get by with a package of peanuts and a bottle of pop on some bright theory that you "do better on an empty stomach"; you don't. Treat yourself. And have lunch as early as you can so as to get it settled before work.

5. *Plan the rest of your lunch hour too.* (a) If you are the type who can nap, fifteen minutes is often a great refresher; but try beforehand to find some place where you can stretch out in reasonable quiet, even if only on the grass; head on arms on a desk, if well adjusted for comfort, is better than nothing; dozing slumped down in an easy chair or other makeshift is often worse than nothing; (b) then a short, brisk walk may get you alert again; and (c) scanning another pre-chosen topic can fill any remaining time and get the mental wheels moving. Use your own judgment as to what works best for *you;* but use it, and stick with it.

6. Particularly, *don't post-mortem* the morning's exam, alone or in a group. This ritual is popularly supposed to blow off steam; but more often it just blows off energy and gets you rattled.

Furthermore, post-mortem addicts are likely to be the panic-mongers discussed in the following chapter, rather than cool, steady heads who will cool and steady you. If you have a friend of the latter sort, you may find him good medicine; walk or chat with him and *forget* exams. I have already acknowledged the value of the bull session as an educational device. But just now you need refreshment, not supplementary education on an issue closed for the present.

An exception to this rule is with minor, isolated exams or quizzes. Here, with no other upcoming test to compromise, a post-mortem can be of real value in discovering and clinching weak points. Only it must be constructive, with competent people, not a mere calamity-Joe session.

The foregoing procedures have a double value: They get the maximum results from the final days and hours before examination; and they exclude wasteful and outrightly harmful practices. Perhaps the second effect is even more important than the first. If these procedures save you from "blowing" only one exam, or from mutilating several, they can be worth as much to you as many days or weeks of study. Therefore:

In Sum

Carefully plan your pre-exam week, day, and hour; and stick to your plan.

Make your study first a systematic review of over-all pattern and then a sober mastery of methodically selected units. Don't gobble.

Go to the exam like a trained, disciplined athlete going to his big trial at top form, not like a hopped-up kid entering a drag race.

The Greatest Enemy
of Exam Takers: Panic

Examination panic is so important a matter that I am going to give it a chapter to itself. It is undoubtedly the greatest single source of lost marks, greater even than faulty preparation, starting exhausted, or misreading questions; indeed, it contributes largely to these other mark-losers. Yet, believe it or not, panic *can* be controlled by anyone who honestly tries.

I am not talking about examination *tension*. This is natural, inevitable and, when kept within bounds, a good thing—people do work better, for a limited time anyway, when keyed up a bit above normal. So don't worry about that.

But *panic* is something quite different. Its extreme form is probably familiar to you from observation if not (I hope) from experience: The victim spends an almost sleepless night (or nights) of feverish and inefficient work under abnormal pressure; he then enters the examination hall with fixed stare, laboring breath, trembling hands, beaded forehead, and pumping heart, and proceeds to mangle the examination. Such a degree of panic *is* extreme and uncommon, but the same picture in a lesser degree is only too common. The self-defeating foolishness and absurdity of such a state is surely obvious.

But *is* it simply foolishness? *Can* it be controlled, as I say, or is it an emotion, which (by modern doctrines) is supposed to be beyond the control of reason? My only answer is that I have seen a dozen severe cases controlled completely and permanently, and numerous mild cases fade away under sane treatment. Here are some of the methods used:

Causes of Panic

Psychiatry tells us that the best way to deal with mental disturbance is to face its causes squarely. Then, if real, a cause can be dealt with by removing it or learning to cope with it or, if illusory, by letting it spontaneously evaporate. Examination panic is certainly a mental disturbance; nine times out of ten its cause is illusory, and the tenth cause is usually simple to deal with. Among these causes are:

1. *Real incompetence* is the least common of the common. Certainly, a consciousness of inadequate preparation might be expected to result in a more or less panic approach to an examination. Yet frequently a weak student approaches the test with nonchalance or stoicism, whereas his brilliant, overprepared classmate experiences panic. Hence the former does better and the latter worse than might be expected. Put yourself on both sides of this picture, and draw your own conclusions. Preparation *plus* coolness is the ideal.

2. *Supposed incompetence* is rather more common. It arises from exaggerated perfectionism, which feeds on itself to produce a feeling of inadequacy. The student with this attitude is so aware of the vast amount of knowledge available in a field that he loses all perspective on what should, and will, be expected of him in practice. Usually also he is fussy and nit-picking so that minor forgettings and omissions loom out of proportion in his mind; and he distorts his paper by crowding early questions with excessive detail and then having to rush later questions so that his panic helps to justify itself by erratic performance—of which he is acutely aware. Thus, his delusion builds up.

3. *Social sheep-following* is certainly far commoner than either of the foregoing—perhaps the commonest panic-builder of all. It arises from a pose prevalent in many quarters, that a show of panic is the smart, swagger thing, proving that you are not a "square" but a regular guy. This pose infects the imitative student who conforms to the crowd and apes the fashionable role. Then he, in turn, helps to infect other impressionable classmates in a vicious circle, building up the atmosphere of tension. But acting a

part infallibly means falling into the part in reality (as professional actors know) usually to a minor though harmful degree, but sometimes quite realistically. Then the pose becomes a real, devastating panic.

The truth, that panic is infectious, is proved when one compares classes in different years. In some, two-thirds of the students show obvious signs of excessive tension, quite evidently spreading from a small number of panic-mongers; other classes show a noticeable, mature calmness that dampens down the few panic-mongers themselves. The difference can hardly be due to a chance flood of hypertensive people one year and a lack of them the next. It can only be due to a relatively small difference in the percentage and personal impact of panic-mongers.

In this connection, beware the alarmist upperclassman. This type delights in telling fearsome stories to newcomers, whether to raise his own prestige, or from a sadistic sense of humor, or for some more obscure reason. "Old So-and-so once ploughed *thirty per cent* of a class—and made it stick! . . . If Dr. Such-and-such gets his knife into you, watch out! ! . . . Mr. Blank sets questions on stuff that he never touches in lecture! ! ! !" Such fables will be dealt with below. Meantime, take it for granted that your "informant" is a smart-aleck, if no worse.

4. *Posing* is not confined to public conformity; it can be done for one's own gratification. Some people seem to take positive pride in how scared and tense they can make themselves: "See how I strain every fiber of my soul! I run scared! Observe how passionately I feel my situation! Surely I deserve top billing!" But nothing earns top billing except top performance, and top performance is not promoted by panic. And the pose often gets the upper hand as uncontrolled panic.

Or the pose may be a sort of alibi. In case of failure or near failure, it allows one to say, "See? I told you so," to oneself and to others. Which is simply helping oneself to do poorly for the pleasure of being right about it.

Or the pose may be a sort of placation of jealous gods. Consciously, the poser would be as ashamed to admit belief in such, as he would be to carry a four-leaf clover. But deep down he harbors the classic Chinese belief that one can avert bad luck by self-deprecation. Observably, however, any real Powers Above reward merit, not panic posing.

5. *Overmotivation* is due to various causes. Some of these are, at least in theory, admirable, and some are deplorable, but all open the way to panic. The overmotivated student may plan to put the world to rights; or he may have glowing ideals of his intended profession, or a true but undisciplined thirst for knowledge and achievement; or he may be too fixated on his immensely important goal rather than on the job in hand; or he may want to "show" somebody or bodies for personal reasons; or he may simply be highly competitive; or he may combine any or all of these drives. In any case, he develops a habit of flogging himself to the limit and of taking examinations too intensely to heart. But such habits are self-defeating: They produce stunted results compared to a balanced, mature approach.

6. *Feedback* is really not a basic *cause* of panic, but an aggravation of *all* the basic causes. This term is used in engineering to describe a self-promoting process: Say, a valve in a pipe lets a trickle of water through, but the trickle acts on a mechanism to open the valve further, which increases the flow, which increases the opening, and so on in an accelerating build-up. Just so, the types of panic-builder listed above react unfavorably on a student's performance: His supposed inadequacy produces strenuous but misguided efforts, neglect of health, and mental turbulence; which result in inadequate performance in examinations; which reinforces his lack of confidence; and so on in a spiral. If he is a competent student, he may keep going with a certain degree of credit, but at a ruinous cost in health, pleasure, and final achievement; really brilliant people of my acquaintance have needlessly worn themselves down by overtension into mere good second- or third-raters by the time they took their degrees. Weaker students tend to follow a steeper spiral which leads them to extreme panic and disaster. This snowballing kind of feedback is called *positive* in engineering parlance.

Naturally the development of panic is rarely as simple as the foregoing examples might imply. Causes are compounded: The overmotivated student has also an alibi-pose of being scared and a nagging fear of incompetence; the sheep-follower not only gives way to fashionable panic but compounds it with real incompetence due to foolish study and other habits; the student with a fixation on his goals also fears not "showing" his family and friends; and so on. Thus, panic is an insidious thing, and hard to pin down.

What to Do About Panic

But if you face things squarely, you *can* pin down the sources of panic. And once pinned, you *can* deal with them.

1. *What you have built up you can break down.* As remarked above, natural tension is always there, more or less in different people, and should be accepted. But the build-up, the feedback, has been due to your own inexperience, delusions, and misconceptions; and if you recognize these for what they are, you can reverse the feedback to a *negative* form—an increasing "flow of water" turns the valve *down,* and restricts the flow to a desired amount. Negative feedback is just as simple and natural as positive; or even more so because you are firmly directing it.

2. *Don't expect immediate, miraculous results.* Probably you have been building up your panic for a long time; and whereas organized treatment will repair the damage more rapidly, you *will* require a certain amount of time for the treatment to take effect. True, I have seen people subdue panic almost overnight by simply making up their minds to it; but these were very unusual people, and their panic was due to peculiar circumstances and was not deep-seated. Ninety-nine per cent of us would experience only frustration and discouragement in such an endeavor. In general, if you can once tackle an examination with a *somewhat* calmer mind, and achieve *somewhat* better results, you have your trouble on the defensive; you see that you can do it, and have started your negative feedback. If you now stick with it, you will do even better next time and will soon be back to normal.

3. *Go about it practically.* In line with (2) above, do not expect results from a simple effort of determination: "I *will* overcome this weakness." This, by itself, is as ineffectual as "willing" yourself to remember. Certainly, you must apply steady determination to achieve success in either endeavor; but it must be supported by practical procedures. The will power should be applied to making sure you carry out these procedures as follows:

4. *Use planned study to strengthen confidence.* The instinctive reaction to poor performance is to redouble effort; but this usually fails to achieve the desired results since mere brute effort is inefficient and exhausting; often it even reacts adversely, with a positive feedback. On the other hand, with planned study you know you have covered the work systematically. You have pat-

terned knowledge: Your material is laid out clearly, even if not perfectly, rather than as a vague discouraging confusion with exaggerated gaps. Above all, the habit of written play-back brings you into the examination firing line with a confidence born of practice and experience; you *know* you can do it because you often *have* done it.

Of course, your emotional subconscious may not accept your new-won improvement as being "real" till you have demonstrated its reality once or twice. But as soon as you establish negative feedback, even the essentially stupid subconscious will begin to lose its panic.

5. *Avoid panic-builders.* Shun the pre- or between-examination panic bull session: "Oh brother, was that a stinker! I don't know how I'm going to get through chem, and that's going to be even worse. How about you?" Or if you cannot gracefully withdraw, look with cynicism not on the examinations being discussed but on the bull-shooters: After all, what is *their* opinion worth? It is mostly swagger and alibi anyway. Better associate with the quiet, cool-headed, say-nothing types. You can learn maturity, and other things, from them.

Refuse to dwell on errors and omissions in past examinations: They always loom many times larger than they really were. Consider rather the goodly amount of satisfactory work you accomplished—backed up by knowing that you have followed a systematic study and examination plan. By all means, you should try *later* to analyze the reasons for lapses (other than the simple fact that nobody can know everything), including panic itself, and figure out how you can avoid them in future. But otherwise, firmly dismiss post-mortems from your mind and focus on the next trial.

As you prepare, especially in the final days, do not dwell on disturbing motives: "Oh, what'll my Old Man say about it if I blow this one? . . . What would So-and-so think if I don't rank high? I'll show him (her)! . . . Two years' hard work all shot just for one stupid, unessential course. . . ." These things can indeed spur you on, often excessively, but they will poison your efforts if you give them a chance. Your study habits play a part here: Mass-assault studying, besides everything else, leaves you vulnerable to unpleasant wool-gathering; study-unit work and mental recall keep you too busy and make you too healthily tired for morbid worry. If you cultivate a sturdy lawn, you cut down on weeds.

6. *Debunk myths.* That professor who failed 30 per cent of his

class—is it true or, even if so, was it due to some extraordinary cause such as a cheating scandal? Realize that excessive failures reflect seriously on the examiner, especially if he is also the instructor; his methods of examining and/or teaching will soon be called into question by higher authority. Some examiners are, indeed, barking dogs but they are held on a short leash: One that I know of habitually sets examinations that *do* fail a third of his class, but he then has to pro-rate results to put grades where they would be if he set more realistic questions. You *may* be in the lower 30 per cent of the class; but *are* you in the lower 7 or 8 per cent that is the highest normal mortality? Be sensible. Stop believing in bogy-men, and thereby help yourself to stay out of that 7–8 per cent.

The myth that some examiner is out to "get" you is so silly as to be incredible—except that it periodically crops up. Thus, I was once told of a student who was in a blue funk because *I* was "laying for him." As a matter of fact, I was hardly aware of his existence and had been giving average grades to him as a neutral figure in a large class. But some routine incident had evidently been magnified by a fevered brain into a mortal threat. Thus the panic fever had exerted positive feedback. This case, I think, is typical.

Such improbable myths are the offspring of immaturity. Look at them rationally as an adult, and dismiss them.

An examination is, indeed, a crisis—but only a very mild one if you have prepared faithfully and well. It should be regarded as a challenge to be met with mature resolution, not a terror to arouse panic unworthy of even a bright child. So regarded, it can even add zest to life.

In Sum

Panic disastrously undermines success and satisfaction.
Panic is always irrational and self-made.
It can always be controlled by a normal person.
Control should be practical and progressive.
This depends *first* on recognizing its sources, *second* on re-establishing confidence by rational means, and *third* on banishing foolish panic-builders.
After which, negative feedback will do its work.

15

The Examination: Attacking Any Paper

Why Examination Techniques?

You have studied your best over the long and the short term. You have put yourself into the best physical condition and the coolest mental state possible. Now you face the "moment of truth," the examination paper before you.

What you do during the next hour or two will have as much effect on your standing as will everything you have done before. This is speaking not just of the material you present but of your technique: A masterly grasp of the subject can be largely offset by faulty presentation; whereas a comparatively mediocre knowledge can be made quite impressive by astute handling. Certainly, good and bad scholarship must weigh heavily, however expressed. But the ideal is obviously good scholarship *and* good technique.

The average student fails to recognize this fact adequately. He comes to examination like a soldier who goes into battle with all the ammunition he can carry but who has never learned how to shoot. He may even feel that a studied approach to examinations is above his head, too much trouble, and not really necessary, that he needs only to dig in and blaze away as he has always done; all of which is far from the truth. A sophisticated approach can make a 10 to 20 per cent difference in grades. And in real life, beyond the examination hall, the successful man is not the one who merely "knows"—who is more likely to be only an expert underling. He is the man who knows *and can apply* his knowledge, who can "put it across." People are tested for this ability, as well as for knowledge, by examinations.

In the following pages, you will find a good deal of advice. How, you may wonder, are you supposed to bear it all in mind and put it into practice in the heat of an examination? The answer is, of course, that it should have become second nature to you long before you face the examination. You should have been "learning to shoot" all along. In discussion of study units and review, you were repeatedly reminded of examinations ahead; and every time you have performed play-backs, you should have been rehearsing examination (and real life) situations up to hundreds of times. Therefore, this and the following chapters should be only a pre-exam refresher on many points.

The present chapter deals with effective approach to any examination. It is introductory to both Chapter 16 on subjective "essay-type," Chapter 17 on objective "short-answer" examinations, and Chapter 18 on oral examinations.

Examination Planning

First, size up that paper like a seasoned general sizing up his enemy.

The type of student I would call a Plunger is familiar to all. As the papers are handed out, he sits tensed, pen or pencil quivering in his fingers. He seizes his paper, peers at it feverishly, and begins to write at top speed almost before his eyes leave the first question. (Less extreme forms of plunging, such as impetuously muttering down the whole paper, without really reading anything, are only a little less idiotic.) By this inspiring show of zeal, he may save fifteen or twenty seconds; and very likely he squanders fifteen or twenty minutes by one or more of the blunders noted in this and the following chapters. He is dime-wise and dollar-foolish.

Size up that paper. Resolve in advance to spend a definite time, two or three minutes, for planning your campaign. Indeed, some counselors advise spending quite a lot longer, but I do not think this is necessary if you have adequately rehearsed examinations in study play-backs; you should very quickly see how the land lies. Do not, however, simply read the questions and select one to start with. Calculate how to make the best over-all showing.

1. *Budget your time:* Few examination blunders are so common

as failure to allow enough time for a perfectly good question. This is due to lack of plan.

Suppose, for the simplest example, you have an essay-type exam with four questions and an hour in which to answer them. One question is undoubtedly your meat; two are about average; and one rather daunts you. How do you budget time? Aside from very special circumstances, budget twelve minutes apiece with twelve over for margin (of which you have already spent two or three for planning). That sounds rather rigid but the schedule *may* be adjusted for those special circumstances.

One cause for readjustment is absolutely *not* the relative difficulty of the questions:

Suppose you give extra time to your "good" question. Now, in the allotted twelve minutes you may easily earn 22 or 23 of the possible 25 marks, leaving only 3 or 2 to gain even if you give five minutes more to this question. Whereas your "bad" question may net you 18 marks if you give it all you can, but can easily fall to 12 or lower if you give it up as a bad job and starve it of time. Thus you are gambling maybe 1 or 2 extra marks against maybe 6 or 8—a bad bargain.

To feed your bad question at the expense of your good is equally unwise. Assuming that you are really weak in the former, your information *is* limited, and extra time will produce only trivial scraps and profitless padding (see page 144). Therefore, tackle the question manfully in the ways to be described; put down all you can dig up in the allotted time, which may be more than your pessimism expects; and drop it without penalizing your other work. This is good strategy.

The average questions will naturally command average time automatically.

A legitimate "special circumstance" for adjusting question times is the use of some short-cut. In the well-known Chinese proverb, "One picture is worth a thousand words." If you have learned diagrams, pictures, tables, and such, you can probably present them in less time (and with better effect) than a long discourse— even when they are not specifically called for. In that case, allocate the time saved where you think it will get most results, not just at random.

If questions are not of equal value, a little mental arithmetic will tell you how much time to give each—always leaving that margin of safety. But double-check those times to make sure that they fit into your hour and are really proportionate; under examination stress, one can make strange, and costly, errors. Even so, all this should take hardly a minute.

Note that besides its other benefits, this procedure insures you against omitting questions. Incredible as it seems, this blunder is not uncommon, especially when more than three or four questions are set, or for part of a subdivided question. And it is the most disastrous of blunders: A charitable examiner can give you some credit for a misread or misanswered question but what *can* he do about one not answered at all? When you are following a strict schedule, any omission makes itself promptly evident: How is it that you have ten more minutes than you thought?

2. Decide in *what order* you will take the questions. This procedure will take the rest of the minutes budgeted for planning. The order chosen will depend largely on your personality in examinations, about which you should have learned a good deal during study-unit play-backs. Probably you should start with the hardest question, while you are fresh, not with the easiest (for you) which is apt to carry you away. Finish with the easiest, in which you have a surplus of material; then you can gain nearly full marks even if you leave some out due to fatigue and lack of time. In any case, *plan* your program, and stick to it.

3. Then *work with your watch in front of you*. Many people do this to keep check on total exam time; but you should time each question strictly. Paavo Nurmi, the great runner, always ran against his own clocked record for each phase of a course, not against his competitors; and you should do likewise. Particularly make sure that you are not eating into your margin of spare time by more than a minute or so. Conscientious study-unit play-back should have trained you in the technique of handling material in strictly limited time. Do not break training now in the crisis; make it work for you.

Read the Question

Your first reading was for general plan. Now you focus on one question.

Misread questions are a very common source of lost marks. The tragedy of this is that, almost always, the loss is totally unnecessary; for lack of a few seconds' attention, many hours' worth of devoted study are sacrificed and an answer that could have netted you high or at least adequate marks becomes mediocre or worthless. How do you avoid this?

1. *The deadly trio, fatigue, panic, and plunging,* are the source of most misreading. Here (as well as in the body of the answer, but even more fatally) that extra hour or two of worthless self-flogging the night before, that heroic martyred pose, that jack-rabbit take-off, penalize their deluded victim. The loss of half, or most, of even one question from these causes can seriously or totally compromise your standing. So, contemplate the sections in this book on physical self-discipline (Chapter 4), panic (Chapter 14), and plunging (see above) in the light of that blunt fact, and ask yourself: "Is this advice theoretical preaching or basic common sense?"

2. *Train yourself to read the question.* Do not just stare at it as if pure physical tension would squeeze the juice from it. Learn to probe rapidly but critically, to question the question: Could it mean *anything other than* your first impression? (For example, in answering: "Discuss the effect of the Diesel engine on modern transportation," a number of frantic candidates will present an excellent, and quite irrelevant, description of how the engine works.) Does it mean *more* than that impression? (In answering: "Describe the mineral resources of Barataria," a similar number will give metals but omit coal, commercial stone, and so on.) Does it mean *less?* (In answering "Describe the blood supply of the brain," the same inaccurate type will waste much time on veins, which are not "supply" but drainage.) Why is a question *phrased* in a rather odd manner? A good examiner frames a question with care to mean exactly one thing and nothing else; he must do so if only to avoid being presented with legitimate alternative answers which greatly complicate his task of fair grading. He also must frame the question so as not to give away too much; so you can wonder: What is he trying to make you infer? Focusing in these ways also tends to eliminate other errors such as misread words. It makes you stop and think.

Another approach to interpreting questions is: Does the question, as you read it, seem *unreasonably* difficult or easy for the time available and the marks allotted? In either case, you had better look sharply at your interpretation.

Let me re-emphasize: You cannot think of all these things quickly unless you have practiced doing so in your course of study. But if you *have* practiced, they should all take hardly another minute of your time per question, and are richly worth it. Therefore, practice them on every old exam paper available till they become automatic.

3. At the same time, *don't try to be oversubtle.* The examiner, again in his own interests, will also set his question to be straightforward and usually on some important aspect of the subject; he will not set sly traps or go far out in left field to fail 30 per cent of the class and thus lower his own reputation. Only if he is incompetent will he express himself obscurely. A competent examiner will not appreciate hair-splitting on your part even if technically justified—which it probably will not be. Be sensible and practical in your interpretation.

4. If in spite of all precautions the question remains obscure, *ask.* Do not be bashful but tackle the examiner himself or, if he is not there, at least the proctor: "Does the question mean *this* or *that?*" (never "What does this mean?"—a plainly unfair demand). He can't eat you; he can only refuse to give more information and tell you to use your judgment. In that case you at least gain the hint that the ambiguity is probably in your own mind, not in the question as written; if it were the latter, he would be bound to admit it. On the other hand, if the ambiguity is real, you *may* do yourself (and the class, and even the examiner) a big favor by pointing it out.

5. As a last resort if ambiguity persists, *say so on your paper— tactfully,* not as if criticizing the examiner. Thus: "I interpret this question to mean such-and-such, not so-and-so." A fair examiner may then say, "Yes, I see his point, and he has acted not from ignorance but from judgment, and he appreciates the alternative." This may be worth some consideration for you even if you are wrong.

6. Unit-study, as described in Chapter 10, will not help you in reading questions. But it *will* do so if you make a further practice of titling your units as if they were exam questions. This, by forcing you to share the examiner's problems, will help you to read his mind on exams.

This chapter can raise your grade substantially, even save you failure, *before you set pen to paper.* And all at the cost of only a little restraint rather than plunging. But of course, restraint is of small use if you have not practiced how to use the time.

In the next chapter we will discuss how to improve your grades further by simple techniques when you *do* start writing.

In Sum

An examination can yield far better returns to professional treatment than to haphazard, amateur bungling of the same material.

Treatment should begin with a deliberately thought-out schedule to be followed rigorously. Time the questions, arrange them in effective order, and budget a margin of safety.

Each question, as you come to it, should be read critically from several angles: Does it mean something different, something more, or something less than your first impression? Does unusual phrasing mean something? Does the question seem suspiciously easy, or unduly hard, and if so, why? But do not split hairs.

If a question seems ambiguous, ask about it or note the ambiguity on your paper.

Mastering the Examination:
Subjective Type

The subjective or essay type of examination is not so universal as it once was. It is a quite impractical form for very large classes and for examinations dealing with candidates from many institutions or even nationwide. Thus, it is used most often for smaller classes, and is generally set by the person who taught the material. These facts have bearing on the way such exams should be handled.

I have pointed out that the purpose of study is to carry away knowledge. Exactly so, *the purpose of taking examinations is to display that knowledge to best effect.* Both statements seem quite obvious, but the one is as widely disregarded as the other. As rituals are often substituted for effective learning, so too they replace effective treatment of examination questions. Yet effective treatment is supremely important in subjective exams.

However, a student rarely presents the best answer possible even *for him*. Rather he impulsively follows one or more traditional formulas: He fills as many books as he can, no matter with what; he tries to display a flowery, pompous, and (he fancies) impressive style; he goes to great lengths to camouflage ignorance, real or imagined, with padding and double-talk; at best, he shovels in as many "facts" as he can scrape together, regardless of priority or organization. These methods must be endured (but are never really welcomed) by examiners; otherwise, they would make our schools and colleges echo with vacancies. But such tactics cannot get the best results even for a good student, much less for one in trouble. What then?

The Human Factor

The following suggestions, as I am well aware, are more open to objections than those given elsewhere. These objections could come from two sources, students and examiner.

As regards students: In a recent book, beliefs of graduate students regarding examination requirements were contrasted with faculty recommendations. The divergence was often wide: For example, a great majority of the students felt that the longer the answer, the more effective it would be, but only a minority of the faculty agreed; only about a quarter of the students, but 100 per cent of the faculty stressed well-organized answers; and so on. Such divergence shows how even advanced students can have delusions on examination techniques.

Certainly the students were not entirely wrong. In the first place, instructors sometimes recommend one policy, for the record, and follow quite another in practice. But this is not common; and in this book, anyway, I am speaking objectively and recommending what *I* believe from experience to be the best procedures. And for another thing, the opinions may diverge only in appearance: Long answers, for example, *are* desirable, *if* the length is made up of solid meat, not of padding. The suggestions given here must be interpreted with common sense.

As regards examiners: You should know your man. Many instructor-examiners have preferences, reasonable or not. For instance, one man may object to numbered subheadings; another, to terse composition; and yet another may set high value on a formal introductory outline. Knowing such things may profit you substantially; so, study your instructor for hints on what he likes.

Nevertheless, such preferences need not cancel good examination techniques. Thus, *do not* number your subheadings, but see that proper order is followed *and* indicated in some other way; *do* keep away from time-wasting verbosity, but equally avoid a jerky, "telegraphic" style; *give* your man his outline, but arrange it so that you can fill it in without wasteful repetition. I am quite sure that any examiner, whatever he says, will prefer a concise, clear, straightforward presentation to a flowery, vague, rambling one.

Remember, he certainly will not object to any easing of his dull task, in grading papers, so long as his pet prejudices are not affronted. Thus you can have the best of things both ways.

Adapt Your Style to the Examination

Time is of the essence: You are *not* writing a book. You are *not* writing a term paper. You are *not* writing even an impromptu exercise in English composition. Of course, good form, good English, arrangement for maximum impact, are very desirable qualities. But you must adapt them to the fact that you *are* writing an examination, in which time is a dominant problem. Exam presentation is a distinct form of composition with the following major requirements.

1. *Omit the ceremonious build-up.* You have probably been taught in English composition to begin with a topic paragraph, to "tell them what you are going to tell them," and this is indeed good policy for literary purposes. But on an examination you have no time for more than the most concise introduction—unless you are writing English composition!

For example: The question is: "Discuss the role of naval operations on the Great Lakes in the War of 1812." The dutiful student begins by copying the question in full, a couple of wasted lines. He then launches out somewhat as follows: "In dealing with the War of 1812, sight is often lost of the role played by the not inconsiderable naval operations carried out on the Great Lakes. The effect of these campaigns on the course of hostilities was fourfold. First they affected troop movements. Secondly . . ." This may sound very correct and pretty, but in fact it is about eight (script) lines of waste motion; even the four headings will have to be repeated in the body of the presentation. With the title, this totals maybe ten lines of shadow-boxing.

Instead, *come out fighting.* Omit the title (of which your examiner is probably pretty tired when he reaches your paper), but do indicate the question number clearly—"QUESTION III." Then: "In the War of 1812, naval operations on the Great Lakes had a fourfold influence." (A completely sufficient title and topic paragraph of hardly two lines.)

Then proceed: *"First, invasion* depended on command of the waterways. Major examples were . . ."* Here is your first subheading with solid facts coming up, in two more lines. And no wasteful repetition.

Ten lines rather than four means six wasted. Six times four questions makes twenty-four lines; a full page of writing wasted on this one extravagant display!

2. *Avoid long-winded language.* Someone aptly called this "curly English." Textbooks and other writings indulge in it because they have all the time in the world; and one unconsciously picks up and uses their sonorous phrases. But even in textbooks, such usage is often deplorable; and in an examination, it is always both unsuitable and costly.

"It would seem that in the vast majority of cases a frontal lobotomy on one side . . ." He meant, "Most frontal lobotomies on one side seem . . ." Sixteen words versus seven.

"According to my understanding of the matter, it is generally believed by most authorities that . . ." He meant, "Most authorities believe that . . ." (Obviously this is his "understanding of the matter.") Fifteen words to four.

And so on.

I occasionally go through a paper with a red pencil in the hope of benefiting the writer. In really bad cases, I can strike out even up to a half of the wordage without losing a single mark-earning point. The average, even the good, paper could be trimmed by 10 to 20 per cent in this way. Five to ten minutes out of your hour!

3. *Outlines are conditional.* If you really know your material, an outline is superfluous unless Teacher wants it. Thus it is a sheer waste of time—maybe a substantial waste. By all means you should have an outline in your head, rather than follow blind impulse: For your "War of 1812" question, you should have your "fourfold effects" clearly in mind, probably from some well-remembered study unit. If you feel nervous, you can jot on the back of a page, "Invasion, transport, reconnaissance, prestige" or whatever your headings are. In addition, if some fugitive idea flits across your mind, but you have not reached the proper place for it in your writing, you can nail it by scribbling another word or phrase under the appropriate heading—such things are apt to slip away again, which is maddening. But for a twelve-minute exposition, anything further is usually "more nails than wood."

On the other hand, if you are weak on the topic (or if you have disregarded my counsel and run short of time) an outline may be your salvation. This presumes that you will write *only* the outline with, maybe, a few comments. Thus you reduce the amount of writing, increase the amount of thought, and concentrate on the pattern of the subject, which you should be able to recall even when details elude you. Write it neatly with different notations (A,B,C, . . . 1,2,3, . . . a,b,c, . . .) and indentations for sub- and sub-subheadings; leave blank lines for afterthoughts; leave a good margin to the right for minor comments. If the outline does bring to mind major comments of importance, and you have time for them, don't try to cram them into inadequate space but put them at the end of the question. Try to keep your outline as neat and businesslike as you can.

4. Outline or not, *organization is vital.* As you should not plunge on the whole question, but should size it up, so also, even if more briefly, size up each section. Pause for a moment to clarify what you are going to say; maybe give it a title or topic sentence to focus your mind. This has at least three advantages: (a) Your examiner will naturally be more impressed by a logical presentation than by a jumbled mass. Though he will always try to give you credit for all you present, he will see it more clearly and to better effect if it is intelligently laid out. This is worth marks. (b) Also, you are less likely to waste effort backtracking, repeating, and so on. "Returning to the matter of . . .," "I should have said in connection with . . .," and the like, are confessions of disorganization. Such zigzagging can cost a lot of time, as well as exasperating and confusing the examiner. (c) You are less likely to omit important topics.

If you do have something of importance to add, mark the place with a large asterisk and write in the margin "See below." You should always leave about half a page at the end of every question for just this purpose. If this space does not suffice, say "See back of opposite page," or "See page such-and-such," and number your pages.

Organization is the object of outlines. As discussed above, you should be able to make and hold an outline in your head adequately enough for a short exam question. If you cannot, your study-unit play-backs should train you thoroughly.

5. *Answer the question as given.* If it says "discuss," "list and comment briefly on," "compare," and so forth, do just exactly as directed and nothing else. In particular, if you are asked for a

table, diagram, or other special form, give it. Remember: Marking examinations is one of the world's dreariest jobs, especially for a large class; a "table" or "diagram" question has probably been set to lighten the examiner's load by making at least one item easy to mark. To find instead, on paper after paper, a couple of pages of verbosity is infuriating and could be taken as pure insolence. You are asking for trouble, and deserve it, if you offend in this way whether by oversight or intent.

I can, of course, hear the plaintive cry: "But I'm no artist." or "I never could handle tables." Rubbish: You're not expected to be an artist but merely a clear draftsman—an expectation which any self-respecting person can fulfill. When presented with a childish scrawl of drawing, worth nothing, I have on occasion confronted the culprit with a simple line drawing and ordered him to copy it, which he always found he could do adequately. To me this proves that anyone competent to take higher education can fulfill such routine exam requirements. I submit that the supposed difficulty is purely mental; it is a form of intellectual laziness.

One further caution in such matters: Having made your drawing or table, do not then proceed to repeat the whole business in writing, which is a gross waste of time. You will get nothing but an annoyed glance and not a single extra mark, for maybe five minutes' work. If uncertain that your drawing or whatnot is adequate, spend the time improving *it*.

6. *Don't digress:* People do this for various reasons: They may simply be carried away by excitement; they may be tempted to indulge in something they know well, rather than struggle with something they don't, regardless of what is required; they may even try deliberately to cover up ignorance by a display of misplaced proficiency. Perhaps their conscious or half-conscious thought runs, "I'll get some credit anyway."

But your examiner is not likely to be a fool. He is not going to be taken in by a lot of double-talk; rather, he will probably be annoyed at having to plough through it. Even if he does not downgrade you for being irrelevant or trying to bluff him, he will certainly not give you credit for the stuff. In this way you can waste a sizable part of your time and effort.

You will do better to stop, think, and employ the devices given in Your Salvaged Time, below. In this way you can probably turn up some worthwhile material which will net you more marks than any amount of padding or irrelevancy. So do not try to pad, and do not let yourself be carried away. Stick to the question as you have interpreted it.

7. If you get a mental block on something you know you should know, *don't spin your wheels.* Certainly, ransack your mind for associations, clues and, above all, blanks in the pattern of the subject. But don't sit staring, fuming, and straining. You can leave a corresponding blank, put a distinct mark in the margin so you won't waste time searching for the spot, go on, and let your subconscious mind work. Simply relaxing the tension often lets the missing fact bob to the surface. In this way you save both time and tension.

A Technical Time-saver

In a somewhat different category than the foregoing is *handwriting.*

I am not here stressing only legibility. This, of course, is absolutely essential: If an examiner has to spend double time on your paper, among scores, deciphering your hieroglyphics, he is assuredly not going to give you the benefit of any doubt when his decipherment breaks down. Put yourself in his place and act accordingly when writing your paper. This is obvious.

Incidentally, don't have the impudence to write with a faint pencil. This is as exasperating as an illegible scrawl and will have the same consequences. Use a pen or dark ballpoint.

Less obvious, though equally important, is the time factor. The same students who scribble furiously, to get as much down as they can, very often scribble in an absurdly laborious manner. Some writers can put twice as many words on a page as do others, with equal or better legibility; and these are often among the better students. A pen must cover far more ground to write a word in a big, sprawling, childish script than in a compact one; and the compact writer uses finer, more rapid muscular movements than the sprawler. Thus if you tend to sprawl, you are wasting a sizable proportion of your time. And this will be true not only on examinations but throughout life.

Deliberate effort spent to improve awkward handwriting will therefore pay off. A mere resolution to "do better" is not enough; it is like a resolution to "learn better" without any clear idea of how. Analyze your writing as to why it is so illegible or diffuse, and make up your mind as to what sort of writing you would like to have—maybe some friend's neat, compact script. Then set to work to develop it, not all at once but step by step.

I know that this is possible because I did it myself. From a rounded, copybook script taught me in school, I turned to a much smaller, more economical form. Testing this out, I found I could put down 25 per cent more in a given time than I could previously. My script has since deteriorated but is still fast.

Your Salvaged Time, How to Use It

By the techniques discussed above, the *average* student can save up to half his examination hour! What wouldn't he gladly pay in cold cash for such a doubling of his effective time? Yet once he has it, he may be embarrassed with this riches; long used to filling examination books by desperately scribbling every kind of time-waster, he may feel that terse, compact, meaty presentation only exposes his shortcomings. Wouldn't he be better off to cloak his poverty in a decent fog of verbiage? From this point of view, perhaps he would!

However, I have supplied you with several techniques that can now come to your aid. I have discussed these at length in preceding chapters, and presume you have been practicing them. But I will summarize them here for emphasis:

1. *Patterned* knowledge inevitably means more *available* knowledge. A framework, even faded, will guide you to facts that would otherwise escape you. But it should *not* be faded if pre-exam study has concentrated on major and secondary patterns, rather than on a fevered scramble for nuggets. This is in addition to the aid that patterns give in layout.

2. Even an *arbitrary pattern* (page 82) can guide the examinee to facts. Those five, seven, ten conventional headings, if scrutinized intently, will bring up ideas you might otherwise remember only after the exam. That's what the pattern is for.

3. *"How* do I remember this?" not "I *will* remember it." Didn't you have some good trick for recalling that elusive, vital material? Maybe you cannot even recall the trick itself. But, experience shows, you are more likely to retrieve it than bald material. Especially if you . . .

4. Give your *subconscious* a chance to work here too. Focus on the pattern, seek clues, range over the field looking for forgotten tie-ins. Then if you get only an uneasy sense of more material wavering on the brink of recollection, leave a space for it in your answer, go on, trust your subconscious, and you will probably get inspiration. Of course, this works best if you have already practiced it and have developed confidence (pages 72 and 73).

Keep these techniques, and any others you may favor, *consciously* in mind, not just vaguely available. And *use* them—they work.

But, you say, they take time! All your impulse is to be scribbling furiously like everyone else. Sacred tradition says: "Fill those pages; bulk counts most." Don't be silly.

In the first place: Anxiety greatly exaggerates the time expended. The usual pause for scrutiny is not a couple of minutes but only ten or fifteen seconds. (Time fifteen seconds on your watch and see how surprisingly long it is.) If that pause nets good material, isn't it better than empty, or outright wrong-headed, scribbling? Or superfluous, ponderous outlining?

In the second place: Even an examiner who is impressed by volume will be impressed by facts too. Volume, yes; but only as much volume as you can fill with good, red meat.*

Your Margin of Safety, How to Apply It

This is something different from the extra time just discussed. I was very insistent, in the preceding chapter, on your budgeting twelve or so minutes of margin. Now, what do you do with it?

1. You have already spent two or three minutes *sizing up the paper* and *planning* your campaign. (Sizing up and planning individual questions should be done on the time for those questions, not on the safety margin.)

---

* After the history test in my college entrance examinations, my classmates were comparing notes. I can recall it vividly: "I nearly filled two books." "Huh, I did a page over two," "Yeah, but Bud filled two-and-a-half!" Somebody turned to our class shark in history: "What did *you* do?" "Book-and-a-half." Incredulous sneer: "Gosh, I thought you were *good*. You're *sunk*." But he *was* good; he took a gold medal. He was, incidentally, a master of condensation.

2. You will very frequently have *afterthoughts*—important features of topics overlooked in your first survey, which is just as easy to do with an outline as without. Maybe your earlier appeals to your subconscious will pay off. Maybe the realization that you have otherwise done your best will relax your mind, and let new ideas come through. Such ideas are often worth extra marks.

Two cautions in this matter: First, be sure the afterthought *is* important. Very often, some "P.S." crammed in frantically at a question's end is really trivial or irrelevant—or has even been covered in what was already written! Don't waste your precious margin in this way.

Second, as already recommended, always leave plenty of space for afterthoughts at the end of every question. Never finish one question and begin another on the next line or so. As already recommended, use an asterisk, a specific page reference, and another, *numbered* page if the space is inadequate.

3. Next, *check your questions* against the examination sheet. If you have budgeted your time properly, you are very unlikely to have overlooked a whole question. But where questions are subdivided into (a), (b), (c), etc., one division is amazingly often overlooked. I am inclined to think that, in many cases, this is what they call a "Freudian slip"; that is, a person subconsciously skims over something distasteful. Don't let your subconscious, a good servant, be a bad master in this respect and cost you substantial marks. In case of such an omission, you will be thankful to have your safety margin.

4. After, and only after, these procedures, use any remaining time to scan your answers for *minor omissions, errors, and confusions.* When I was myself an examinee, I rarely failed to salvage several marks in this way. A rapid, but not fevered, reading is apt to turn up something.

In this last matter, however, one caution is classic: *Never change your original answer on impulse,* but only for some good and definite reason—only if you *know* the original is wrong. At the end of an examination, even the steadiest and best-organized student is liable to be a bit erratic. And, as all examiners can testify, his chances are three to one of impulsively changing a good answer to a bad one. People incline to gnash their teeth over corrections they did not make, without ever thinking of the "uncorrections" they refrained from committing, which are far more numerous. You can save marks by scanning and detecting real flaws. But *if in any doubt at all, let the original stand.*

Also do not, in the pressure of the last few minutes, spoil your corrections or additions by making them illegible. If available space is too cramped for corrections, use the advice given above (page 146) for other afterthoughts. Hasty alterations can spoil even what you have already written.

Thus, aside from valuable planning, your margin may be worth more than any other equal part of your examination time. If you use it systematically, not just to leaf back and forth looking for "something," it can be rich pay-dirt.

In Sum

On subjective examinations, beyond everywhere else, thought and organization make a vast difference. The contrast is enormous between a scribbled mass of miscellaneous "facts" presented in the clumsiest style and the vaguest of orders, and a pithy, clear-cut, to-the-point, well-thought-out presentation.

On examinations, time is the vital factor. Therefore:

Practice a concise, clear style in unit play-backs, and use it on examinations.

Omit superfluities, "curly" English, disproportionate outlines, digressions, and all such things.

Organize.

Answer the question in the form required.

When in difficulty, don't spin your wheels, but let your subconscious work.

Practice a legible but economical handwriting.

In these ways, you can save up to half your examination time. Use it well by:

Relying on patterns,

Recalling memory aids,

Calling on your subconscious (again) to find neglected material.

You should always budget, and rigorously preserve, a margin of safety. Use it to:

Size up the paper and plan your attack at the beginning,

Add afterthoughts of importance,

Make sure you have omitted nothing,
And, only finally, scan for minor defects.
But never change an answer on impulse, only for positive reasons.

In conclusion, let me be repetitious for the sake of urgent emphasis: The time to study and first apply your "Rifleman's Manual" is not when the enemy assault is rolling toward your foxhole; at that time, you should be firing with deadly and *automatic* accuracy. Only practice makes perfect—and builds confidence. For that one reason, if no others, practice, practice, practice study play-backs, seriously, critically, intensively. Look forwards to the showdown outlined above.

Mastering the Examination:
Objective Type

On objective examinations, much of what was said for subjectives applies, but with adjustments. The emphasis changes.

General Rules

1. *Rehearsal* is as essential for objective examinations as for any type, but is more inconvenient. It demands enterprise.

You cannot just practice play-backs: They give you the material but no exercise in the special techniques of presenting it. You have to get books of old or model examinations if they are available in the subject. Do not use these as a casual study aid, making a half-hearted attempt to answer each question and then looking up the answer. In this way you may learn a little out of the vast reservoir of available detail; but you will learn a great deal more if you use the papers properly. That is, you should use them as tests under examination conditions—closed books and limited time—when you feel you are ready for it. By this method, you will gain proficiency in general performance and in the special techniques presented below; you will really find out how strong or weak you are, over-all or in particular topics; and you will very positively learn the items that you miss.

If such ready-made material is not available, you and others can set each-other questions. Or if even that is inconvenient, you can prepare questions as you study during the term, and try to answer them towards exam time when they have grown cold. You should practice all types of short-answer questions, but concentrate on the more difficult types. By setting your own questions, you gain an extra bonus: a valuable insight into the tricks of short-answer exams.

2. *Systematic study,* not piecemeal browsing, is just as important for objective as for subjective examinations. True, you will be called on to produce only isolated items of information. But since these will be drawn systematically from the examiner's over-all picture, obviously you will be better able to match them from an organized mental file, a pattern, than from a mental rag-bag. This is why piecemeal study from old exam papers is not only a waste of good self-testing material, but inefficient. So likewise, if you are making up your own questions, wait till you have grasped the pattern of the subject and can relate them to it. In this way, you will be following more closely the procedure of a good examiner.

3. *Plan your campaign* when you face the paper. Closely timing 100 or more short questions is impractical; but you can allot time for each major section according to difficulty. For example, 5 questions of one type may require more time for you than 15 of another—as you should know by experience. Decide also in which order to take the sections as you would for subjective questions (page 136) and for the same reasons. Leave a margin for review. Work by watch. You should have become expert in all this by rehearsal.

4. *Reading the question carefully* is a major problem in objective exams. True, any one misinterpretation costs only a mark or two, but a tendency to misinterpret is your most serious danger here. Also, you have far more question-reading to do, and run far more risk of losing your grip from fatigue, monotony, or undue haste. Though most of the questions will be pretty straightforward, you have to make sure of this in every case; and you will find a certain proportion of teasers (see below for types and treatment). Therefore, scrutinize questions *systematically* in somewhat the same way as recommended for subjective-type questions (page 139) but, of course, more rapidly. This, in fact, is your main task on objective exams.

In particular, read the *instructions* for each group of questions very attentively. An error here can cost you dearly in marks, or at least in time. True, you should be familiar with every type of short-answer question; but some variation in the procedure, if you miss it, can throw you badly. Be alert for such variations.

Your resources in successfully reading all this material are: (a) rehearsal, (b) coming to exam fresh and alert, and (c) knocking off for a few minutes to think of something refreshing (preferably resolved on in advance). Never drudge hypnotically ahead when you know you are losing your grip.

5. Use of your *subconscious* for refractory questions is particularly effective on objective exams. You do not have a variety of choice on details, as you do in essay-type work, but must answer to the point every time; yet if you sit and struggle over one two-mark question after another, you will soon be on edge with tension. Therefore, if you have given a question due scrutiny, searched for clues and associations, and feel you have the answer on the tip of your tongue, do not strain; rather, mark it clearly so as not to waste time looking for it, and go on. Very often, the answer will come to you out of the blue; or some one of the other numerous questions will trigger your memory.

Be careful not to overdo this technique, however. If you load your subconscious with a dozen problems, you can confuse it as readily as you can your conscious mind, so that it will deal with none of them. Reserve the method for those questions where you feel you *should* know the answer. Let the others go, to be treated by techniques to be described later.

Now for some points peculiar (or almost so) to objective exams.

Use Common Sense

One might think that short-answer questions left little room for any but factual errors. But examiners are constantly vexed by the frequency with which candidates penalize themselves on apparently foolproof (or even normal-proof) matters. Watch out for the following.

1. Make sure your multi-page *paper is complete.* Incomplete papers are rare, and should be caught by the examiner when he marks them. But even this would cause trouble, and a missing page could well escape a harassed and hasty examiner—maybe penalizing you a dozen points. Checking should take only ten seconds.

2. *Ambiguous notation,* however, is commonplace and loses

some candidates several marks. The examiner stops and stares: "What *is* this one? a 4 or a 7?" (or "a G or a C?" or "an a or an o?" and so on). In such a case, the examiner is obliged to mark the question wrong: the ambiguity may be due to sloppiness or to calculated hedging, but in either case it deserves no leniency. The same is true of putting answers in the wrong place, or setting them so carelessly in the brackets, or on the line provided, that a 3 looks like an 8, or an F like an E. (Script letters, if clear, are often less confusing than print.) Your examiner may stop, peer, and give you due credit; but he may quite unintentionally misread—and the fault is yours.

The remedy is simple: Actual writing-in of letters and figures should take hardly five minutes of your hour; a little extra neatness should take only a minute or two more. This could be the most rewarding minute or two of your whole hour. So avoid indecent, panic haste. (Also eliminate bizarre lettering from your style: flat-topped A's that look like H's, 7s that look like 9s, and so forth.)

3. Use *pencil,* but good black pencil, for your answers; and have a good eraser with you. A mess of cross-outs and superimposed new answers can confuse and delay even you.

4. In *identifying still unanswered or doubtful questions,* avoid all possibility of confusing yourself *or* the examiner. Many examiners use red pencils, so don't you; use green, say, or light blue. For the same reason don't, in any case, use check marks or crosses: either may be used by an examiner to indicate wrong answers! A green circle, say, can confuse no one and is easy to pick up.

Special Techniques for Objective Exams

1. Do not be *overhasty* in writing down your answer. Most people get ahead of schedule anyway, and you have budgeted a margin of safety, so why rush? But why not? Because you will find it far harder to detect and correct a wrong answer once written than to have second thoughts while the answer is still in your head; that visible letter or number looks *so* convincing. Therefore, don't plunge, but do all your thinking before you record it.

Of course, you can be faster with some questions than with others. If a question seems to be a gift, scrutinize it sharply, answer it, and get on; if you ponder feverishly over *every* question, you will soon wonder which of your hands is right and which is left. Put a little more sweat into more doubtful questions, but not too much. A bit longer for some questions will balance a bit shorter for others. Rehearsal should have trained you to know how a group will average out.

If a question defies solution beyond the usual limit, *mark it clearly* (see above) and leave it for your final review (or subconscious). *Don't* put in an answer "for the time being."

2. In line with the foregoing, be very *sparing of corrections* once your answer is down. Corrections are of two sorts: those that follow a realization, based on good reason, that you are wrong; and those where a panic impulse impels you to change. Always make the former, of course; *never* make the latter. This is especially true in objective examinations: Long experience shows the odds are three to one that your impulsive "correction" will be from a right to a wrong answer. Everybody should know this; yet after almost every examination some student reports with anguish how he succumbed to temptation and wonders if he can take back his foolish blunder—which, of course, he cannot. Make an absolute rule of never changing answers *on impulse*. Of course, cases will arise where you find afterwards that you would have been right in making such a change, and these will stand out in your mind; but the three cases where you did not change, and would have been wrong to do so, are there just the same, even if you do not remember them so well. Stick to the rule; you will be ahead of the game on the average.

3. Keep alert for *traps*. On a subjective test, these are unfair and unlikely. On an objective, they are almost necessary, because straightforward questions, stiff enough to separate "the men from the boys," are hard to draw up in large numbers. So the examiner must challenge your alertness.

Even so, they will be fair traps, not booby traps. And they will be apparent to anyone who is awake on the job. Something odd, not quite right, should make you pause like a wary animal who sees the trapper's footprint. Take, for example: "All the following were signers of the Declaration of Independence, *except:* Samuel Adams, John Quincy Adams, John Hancock, Jefferson Davis, Richard Henry Lee. Doubtless you will find the traps in this question obvious, but let's analyze them: Two Adamses did sign, but the second was Samuel—John Quincy was a boy at the time; and Thomas Jefferson can be confused with Jefferson Davis, the

Confederate president of some ninety years later. These are perfectly open traps; but you have to be alert to catch such things.

Scores of examples would be required to illustrate all common forms of trap. The above must suffice to give the general idea.

4. *Arrangement of the questions* may have been of minor use in the past, but is not even that today. For example:

In multiple-choice questions, the first and last choices were supposed to be far more unlikely true answers than the other choices. Or if, say, the second choice was obviously right in one question, it was far less likely to be right in others. Or in matching columns, an item in one column was unlikely to be placed opposite the corresponding item in the other column. And so on for other types of question.

These "guides," never very good, have now passed into the realm of folklore. Today, any examiner of any experience knows the traditions better than his students do, and draws up his paper so that arrangement will be on a strictly random basis. Thus an effort to outguess him along these lines is a waste of time, and may mislead you badly. Forget it.

Use Low Cunning

This is a very different thing from the guessing-game folly described in the last paragraph. The phrase was coined by a high-school teacher of mine to indicate tactics that were not quite academic but that worked. These tactics are only occasionally useful and are no substitute for thought; but they may be worth an odd mark or two. So, they are not to be despised in their proper place.

1. *Give-away words* sometimes solve problems otherwise mere toss-ups. Such positive words as "all," "every," "no," "never," strongly hint that the statement is wrong; just one exception invalidates it, and even if none occurs to you, and if the question *is* a toss-up, you would be playing the odds to choose against the statement. Conversely, hedging words like "usually," "some," "many," or even "most," strongly hint that the statement is true; even if you know of exceptions, are they really important? Again, play the odds and choose in favor of the statement, *if* the answer is uncertain.

2. *Tactics in matching* should be obvious, but are not always used. You have two columns of items and are to put the letter or number of each item in one column, opposite the appropriate item in the other. A good many students work stolidly down the columns, choosing or guessing for each item in turn; or they draw a confusing criss-cross of connecting lines, compounded by corrections. A more astute candidate runs quickly down the list, enters the answers for those items of which he is sure, and marks out the items in both columns clearly but *not* so as to obscure them—he *may* want to recheck later. He then deals similarly with less positive, but probable items. Such elimination may leave only two or three real problems; and for each of these, rather than with four or five to confuse the issue, one answer may stand out as logical, another as absurd. This tactic is less "cunning" than it is honest common sense.

3. *Tactics in multiple-choice questions* are exactly similar, obvious, and frequently disregarded. Eliminate the certainly wrong choices, then the very probably wrong, and concentrate on the remainder.

In both (2) and (3), if hard-core alternatives remain obdurate, don't plunge and don't spin your wheels. Remember what has been said about the stubbornness of answers once written and the advantages of a cooling-off period. Mark the question clearly for prompt recognition on review, and move on.

4. In *completion* questions, where you fill in a blank, watch for hints. You often get a separate dash for each word of the desired answer, even a dash proportionate to the length of the word, thus: "The first amendments to the constitution are known as ⎯⎯ ⎯⎯⎯ ⎯⎯ ⎯⎯⎯⎯." Yet the occasional dazed student ignores this kindly guide and scribbles in something like The Appendix. (Again a glaringly obvious example, of course.) Scan down a list of such questions: If the number of dashes varies, good; if not, the answers may all be single words, or the examiner may mean "no hints given." Use judgment: The answers to "safe" questions may help you to decide policy if one of *them* contains several words.

Examples of similar hints are: "Horus was an ⎯⎯⎯⎯ sun-god." Here the answer must obviously begin with a vowel. Yet candidates will write Greek or Norse.

Again. "The syrinx in birds is analogous to the ⎯⎯⎯⎯ in mammals." "Syrinx" might be a foreign plural, but "is" identifies it as singular, and almost certainly not "bronchi" or "gill-arches."

Of course, many examiners avoid such hints ("Horus was a sun-god in _____ mythology."). And the number of marks to be picked up in these ways will be trivial at best. But don't throw them away through lack of alertness.

5. Far more important, but more difficult to apply, is *cross-referencing*. Your examiner *may* touch on a topic twice, just to see whether you are thinking or playing games; but he is unlikely to do so very often—he has too much ground to cover. So, if you find many apparent repeats, be suspicious. Maybe you are interpreting questions incorrectly; or if not, one question may throw light on another, especially one that has given you trouble. This is one advantage of suspending judgment on dubious questions and keeping them in the back of your mind; some later question may trigger a sudden breakdown of some mental block. But you have to be really fresh and alert, not just a plodder, to catch such hints.

Revision

You have been told to reserve a safety margin of spare time. Now, what do you do with it?

1. One thing you should *not* do is to *reread the paper* looking for errors. You can do this, usually with profit, on subjective examinations. But to review scores of brief questions in the short time available results only in ineffectual skimming and mental chaos. The bulk of the questions should be settled as well as they ever will be; and impulsive changes are usually disastrous. Let them lie.

2. But if you have followed instructions, you will have a selection of *unanswered questions*. You should have marked these distinctively so that you lose no time in finding them, and overlook none. These are your present concern.

Now, these questions are likely to be stickers, and you are certainly tired. However, you do now have several advantages: First, you earlier broke away from a mental block that only threw your mind into cramps, but now you can view the question afresh; second, your subconscious mind has had a chance to work, and may be ready with an answer or a good clue; third, later questions may have jogged your memory, offered clues, or eliminated certain material (see above); fourth, you have done the bulk of the paper, know (I hope) that you are at least safe if not outstanding, and are trying only for extra points, so that you can relax somewhat; and fifth, most candidates on short-answer exams find that they have more rather than less margin than they planned. So tackle these questions calmly, systematically, and with a mind open for clues.

3. *Don't* attack them in *rigid order*. A first run-through should eliminate problems that were due only to temporary mental block, and some others. A second run should be more rigorous, and eliminate questions at which you can make an informed or at least strongly intuitive guess. Make it, leave it, and don't fret about it or thresh it over and over.

Finally, let's face it, you will probably have a hard core of complete enigmas. Unless you are very bad indeed, these need not alarm you; surely you did not expect to make 100 per cent! My advice here might be considered improper by some, but it is the only thing practical in the conditions set by such examinations: Make the best guess you can, and write it in. Remember, you have at least a chance of being right; but no-answer is absolutely sure to net you no marks. Of course, some examinations give you minus marks for wrong answers, just to discourage such guessing; and in that case you do not guess but leave a blank. But usually, a paper studded with blank answers is a disaster.

4. Having followed the foregoing procedures, *quit*. Make sure every page is signed (even stapled papers can come apart) and turn your paper in. Some candidates steam-roller through their papers and call it a day—an exaggerated form of "don't change answers"; these papers, scanned by a proctor to while away the time, usually reveal silly flaws that a logical system of revision would have detected. Other candidates cling spastically to the paper to, or even beyond, the last minute; and these usually do change answers for the worse. Have your plan of campaign pre-set, follow it, and walk out, even if you have time to spare.

In Sum

Objective examinations are far from a mechanical exercise. They should be prepared for systematically and handled with logic. In particular:

Rehearsal, though more difficult than for subjective exams, is even more important. This applies particularly to techniques.

Study should be by pattern, not by "nuggets."

Plan your campaign as carefully as for a subjective exam.

Careful reading of material *and* instructions is paramount. Watch for traps. Watch for hints.

Your notations (letters and numbers) should be clear and unambiguous.

For the exam as a whole: Clear up the easy questions first, then those of moderate difficulty. Finally, concentrate on remaining problems; fatigue is more than offset by other factors.

Similarly, in individual questions don't plough straight ahead; eliminate first the obvious, then the problematic, and concentrate finally on the difficult. Unless penalties for wrong answers are indicated, any answer is better than none.

How to fail an examination even while knowing the answers:

1. Arrive in a daze due to an (ineffectual) attempt to "cover" the whole course during the night. Your noble prodigies will placate the Powers Above, whatever the effect on the examiner.

2. Try to counteract the daze by extra coffee, or by pep pills. This will make you feel awfully clever, however scrambled your presentation.

3. Scan the questions in a flash. If you do misread, your answer will be brilliant enough to rate full credit anyway.

4. Plunge straight ahead without plan or schedule, relying on your unerring instinct. If you run short at the end, write "No more time!" and the examiner will pro-rate what you have done.

5. Don't take instructions seriously; for example, if a diagram is required, give three pages of writing instead. You do it so much better, and the poor, stupid examiner will not know the difference.

6. Write with such frantic speed as to be illegible (a faint pencil helps here). The examiner will assume you are correct on points that he cannot read.

7. On objective, short-answer, examinations, make A's that look like H's, C's like G's, 7s like 9s, V's like II's, and so on. Obviously your answer must be right, so anyone can see that you mean A, 7, or whatnot.

8. Spend the time saved by the foregoing techniques, using long-

winded, flowery phrases, digressing, and padding. This impresses an examiner far more than a few extra facts.

9. Put an addition to some question at the back, especially after some blank, unnumbered pages. A reader will instinctively realize that you know more than just the first part.

10. Leave out part of a question. You are too rushed to attend to such details.

11. Do not sign your paper. The examiner will rather enjoy a little break from routine, trying to identify it.

18

Oral Examinations

Oral examinations, like the essay type, are not nearly as common as they once were. With large modern classes, they require too much time and are too hard to standardize. Yet they are still met with, especially by candidates for higher degrees; and they are related to real-life interviews for job applications and the like. Therefore a brief comment on the best approach to them may be of use.

1. *Panic* is a major hazard on oral exams. Yet this is more than usually unwarranted. Believe it or not, oral exams are the most human and casual form of all; they give the candidate opportunity to retrieve blunders, to have questions interpreted for him, and otherwise to co-operate with the examiner. Why this form of test should be so feared is hard to analyze.

The fear may be akin to stage-fright. But simple observation should largely dispel that bogy. You are not facing a large audience expecting great things of your performance, but only an examiner or group who care little about delivery or style so long as content is adequate. You do not have to recite a long passage accurately but will be led from question to question—even prodded. You can express yourself in any normal terms. You have no stage directions or "business" to remember. All that is left is a common human hesitation to express oneself aloud; and that can be largely controlled as described in Section 2. So do not let a subconscious fear of public speaking control you. Bring it into the open, recognize its lack of force in your position, and dismiss it.

Remember further: On any exam the examiner's own academic

standing depends on the showing made by his candidates; if he makes an unreasonable slaughter, he is cutting his own throat.* On an oral, he can and usually does make efforts to draw the candidate out, soothe panic, offer leads to the bewildered, and find out what the student knows even in spite of the student's balkiness. An example of this is given below. But even such friendliness somehow often backfires.

This is illustrated by one mature medical practitioner of my acquaintance. This man is still absolutely, and bitterly, convinced that one of our staff went all-out to "get" him on an oral: "That so-and-so had had his knife into me all year, and he did everything he could to twist me up." My friend could give no reason *why* Dr. Blank wanted his blood, except capricious spite. Dr. Blank is a mild, kindly man, and a skilled examiner (who could easily have failed the student by subtle means, had he wished); and when indirectly probed on the matter, he did not even recall the victim on whom he was supposed to have waged such a vendetta. I myself have spent most of an exam session calming grown men and women, normally on friendly terms with me, to a point where they could even talk coherently. The folly and tragedy of such behavior is obvious.

Therefore, before any oral exam, read Chapter 14 carefully and consider the following further points.

2. *Rehearse* for *oral* examination. If you have studied diligently with book and pencil but never attempted to utter what you know, you need hardly be surprised if you are tongue-tied in the show-down. A much more poorly prepared student who is fluent and prompt is going to outclass you. But why not have both advantages?

Practice uttering what you know. Mutual quizzing with a fellow student is the best method. But a nonexpert questioner, or a merely passive audience, a relation or friend, can exercise you in expressing your knowledge aloud. Or even a mirror can help if you really talk to it; just mental mumbling is no good at all; you must learn to speak out audibly and coherently. Remember, your object is not simply another review of material, or even an exercise in self-

---

* This, of course, may not apply to highly competitive examinations where only one or a few candidates will be accepted. Here, a candidate's maturity and poise are a major factor. All you can do about this is—cultivate maturity and poise. (But see Chapter 14 for a few hints.)

expression. It is to break down a mental block against spoken replies. Do that, and much of your panic will evaporate.

3. *Understand the technique* of oral examinations. Of course, some examiners simply ask question after question, which presents no special problem. But a more astute practitioner proceeds somewhat as follows: He picks a topic, begins with simple questions on it, and builds up the difficulty till he reaches the limits of the candidate's knowledge. Unless the candidate knows more than the examiner, he is *bound* to reach a limit sooner or later. If experienced, he notes with satisfaction how far he came before the pro could stop him. If inexperienced, he will stress to himself the fact that he "failed" at the end on every topic, and build up panic as he goes. Yet the examiner may be thinking: "This fellow is *good*. I really had to stretch to overreach him that time!" So don't worry where worry is unjustified.

4. *Play along with your examiner.* One of the beauties of oral examinations is their flexibility. They are rather like ballroom dancing where one partner leads and another follows. A competent examiner does not try to put his candidate through a mechanical drill, but to draw him out; to do this, he will rephrase questions, offer reasonable hints, or even give his candidate a push over a hump to see if he can go farther beyond. Or he may introduce what seems to be a digression but dawns on an alert candidate as an approach to the subject from a fresh angle. (Unskilled, mechanical examiners are an affliction that must be borne and dealt with as best one can. They are just as bad for your fellow candidates.) If you play up to these tactics, you may give a far better account of yourself than you could on any written examination. This realization should encourage a calm and efficient mood.

Yet many candidates seem to take perverse delight in evading the examiner's help. They react with the panic of sheep toward the sheep dog who is trying to shepherd them to safety—as did my sore-headed friend cited above. Every oral examiner has taken part in many such tragicomedies as the following:

EXAMINER: And who succeeded Julius Caesar to supreme power?

CANDIDATE: Well, there was a sort of lapse before anyone did.

E: Yes, and who was that finally?

C: Well, not Mark Antony. He sort of tried and failed.

E: So?

C: Well, one of the other Caesars, of course.

E (*patiently*): Which one?

C: Um, uh, er.

E (*helpfully*): Look. Two extra months were named for two Caesars, July for Julius. Who was the other?

C (*instead of running rapidly through the months*): Uh, June might be for Junius, but that was Brutus. And January was for the god Janus. Uh, er.

E (*finally worn down*): What month comes after July?

C: August. Oh! You mean *Augustus* Caesar!!!

Burlesqued? Maybe; but not much. And the candidate, thoroughly shaken in his confidence, goes on to further triumphs of inanity. Later, he will be convinced the so-and-so examiner was "riding" him.

5. *Overanswering* is at the other extreme; it is less common and less harmful, but does not do you any good. Thus, the candidate in the example above might have burbled on: "Well Augustus Caesar first, and then seven others—or was that counting Augustus? Anyway, Augustus wasn't really Caesar's—that is Julius Caesar's —heir. He was adopted, and so were several of the others. But I guess that was legal in Rome. So anyway, he was the next." Such a show of zeal *may* impress the examiner; it may also throw him off the line of questioning he intended. And it will certainly impress him less than a series of neat, quiet answers to: "And what claim had Augustus to power? Did he justify that claim?" and so on. Answer to the point concisely, and be alert for the next question.

6. *Alertness,* you see, is supreme on oral examinations. On a written test, one can at least feebly rally and flog a befuddled brain, review what has already been written, and insert afterthoughts. On an oral, you hardly have time for afterthoughts (if you do, by all means try to elbow them in) and are unlikely to have any if you are foggy with fatigue. Fuddle begets more fuddle from which even the kindliest examiner cannot rescue you. This is the real hazard in oral examinations.

Therefore, my last word to you is this: *Even more* than for written exams, go to your oral as fresh and chipper as you can contrive—well rested, properly fed, and sensibly calm. In the last matter, I hope that this chapter will help you materially.

In Sum

Realize that oral examinations are likely to be more fair and human, *not* more terrifying, than any others.

Get ample pre-exam practice in expressing your knowledge aloud to an audience.

Co-operate with the examiner, and understand what he is trying to do.

Approach the exam in top condition.

Epilogue

A summary of the philosophy behind this book may be of value to some readers. This philosophy has proved rather difficult to distill in a few words. However, here are ten commandments:

1. *Don't drift.* Random, impulsive, fitful toil leads you into a swamp of frustration. Only discipline and planning can achieve effective study, review, and application in exams and in life.

2. *Don't settle for unsatisfactory materials*—books, equipment, place of study, notes, even teachers and schools. Choice today is so wide that a very little effort should find you what best suits your needs.

3. Study to learn *now, permanently, the maximum for time and effort spent.*

4. *Study actively.* Passively "covering" material, empty rituals that only put off real learning, and over-elaborate methods waste time that you cannot spare. Work with pencil in hand, critically.

5. *Treat your brain as a physical organ,* not as a magic file that you can cram without limit and without regard for its mechanisms and needs.

6. *Work in short, intensive spans.* Work pressed beyond an efficient span is mostly forgotten, garbled, or outright rejected by the brain.

7. *Practice not "I will remember!" but "How do I remember?"* Seek or devise patterns, make packages, find vivid correlations, concrete examples, and applications, and take advantage even of mnemonics when these turn up.

8. *Rehearse to confirm knowledge.* No actor, soldier, lawyer,

surgeon, athlete, carpenter, or even ditch-digger could master his craft by merely reading about it, however often. Why should you?

9. *Be trained to present your knowledge effectively in the showdown,* whether examination or real-life situation. Rituals, empty words, evasions, bluff, will not help you. But all the foregoing commandments lead up to your "moment of truth."

10. *Consider how you enjoy your work.* This, to me, is the acid test of effective study. So important is it that I shall make it the subject of a brief valedictory.

Here and there in this book, I have spoken of satisfaction and pleasure in study. I can well imagine that many of my readers may admit the satisfaction, even if grudgingly, but will regard the pleasure with some cynicism. I will, therefore, wind up my counsel by a comment on pleasure in study.

We live in an age of growing pressure. Looking around us, we can see that many people gain little pleasure from their work—a sort of glum satisfaction maybe, but real pleasure, no. Most of us seek pleasure in trivialities: The coffee-break, the spectator sport, the cigarette, or, on a more imposing but still trivial scale, the ostentatious car, status, luxuries, alcohol, futile recreations, all things that offer *escape* from our work. We have lost much of the zest that our ancestors seem to have felt in even arduous activity. Our trivial pleasures themselves lack relish.

Thus, most people, from dignified professionals to minor employees, live a joyless rat-race. How much more the student! He is hounded by a demand for credits, by college entrance, matriculation, and professional board examinations, by increasingly ponderous volumes of information to be mastered, by escalating competition, all leading on to an equally harassed postgraduate career. He dully assumes that such is the natural course of life—without trying anything else. He has never even thought of study itself as possibly a pleasure, rather the reverse. From such an attitude, one can gain little warmth and happiness.

Two main roads ahead are open to people in this situation. For one: They can go on qualifying themselves mentally and emotionally to be cogs in the growing machine; they can grind through the scholastic requirements and pick up a sufficient repertory of skills to get along with or even to achieve success—of one kind. And they can maintain sanity by whatever escapes they may fancy; which is like doctoring bad food with excessive spice. What sort of life is it where real work is toilsome and only distractions are pleasant?

For the second resource: One can meet the challenge of modern life with correspondingly modern techniques; and in vigorous mastery of big jobs, one can find supreme and lasting pleasure. To find it, one needs only the determination to discard old, bad habits and establish new, good ones. Then, too, occasional spice itself has keener flavor.

The two types of student are like two men in heavy surf. One struggles, chokes, flounders, exhausts himself, and finally drags himself ashore bruised, gasping, and with no more fight left in him. The other rides a surfboard with skill and delight, and reaches shore triumphant, exhilarated, and ready for anything. Not that surfboard riding can be achieved without many a flounder and bruise; but once achieved, it is glorious sport. What, then, of achievement in the real business of life? Why not join the minority who enjoy such business—even study? The choice is yours.

It can be done, because it *has* been done. Try it. I hope you succeed.

Index